SUFFERING WELL

THE PREDICTABLE SURPRISE
OF CHRISTIAN SUFFERING

Paul Grimmond

D1428124

Guidebooks for Life 👣

Bible-based essentials
for your Christian journey

Suffering Well is part of a series of straightforward,
practical Christian books from Matthias Media that deal
with the important nuts-and-bolts topics that Christians
need to know about as we walk each day with our Master.

Some Christian books are all theory and no practical
application; others are all stories and tips with no
substance. The Guidebooks for Life aim to achieve a
vital balance—that is, to dig into the Bible and discover
what God is telling us there, as well as apply that truth
to our daily Christian lives.

For up-to-date information about the latest Guidebooks
for Life, visit our website: www.matthiasmedia.com

SUFFERING WELL

THE PREDICTABLE SURPRISE OF CHRISTIAN SUFFERING

Paul Grimmond

Suffering Well
© Matthias Media 2011

Matthias Media
(St Matthias Press Ltd ACN 067 558 365)
PO Box 225
Kingsford NSW 2032
Australia
Telephone: (02) 9663 1478; international: +61-2-9663-1478
Facsimile: (02) 9663 3265; international: +61-2-9663-3265
Email: info@matthiasmedia.com.au
Internet: www.matthiasmedia.com.au

Matthias Media (USA)
Telephone: 330 953 1702; international: +1-330-953-1702
Facsimile: 330 953 1712; international: +1-330-953-1712
Email: sales@matthiasmedia.com
Internet: www.matthiasmedia.com

Scripture quotations are from The Holy Bible, English Standard Version®
(ESV®), copyright © 2001 by Crossway, a publishing ministry of Good News
Publishers. Used by permission. All rights reserved.

ISBN 978 1 921896 31 6

Cover design and typesetting by Lankshear Design.

I moved to Sydney in 1990 and became almost instantly involved with the ministry of St Matthias and Campus Bible Study at the University of New South Wales. In the years since then I have had the privilege of watching many brothers and sisters pack up their belongings—and for some of them, their families—and travel to the other side of the world to speak to complete strangers about our Lord Jesus Christ. It has not been easy for any of them, and for some the cost has been particularly acute. In many ways they have been the best example to me of what this book is all about.

They have counted the cost, lived for Jesus, and encouraged me by their example to suffer well.

This book is for them.

CONTENTS

Chapter 1

THE REAL PROBLEM

Simon steps into the swimming complex. The humidity is a relief after the dry chill of the early morning air. The soft lights welcome him in out of the blackness he wakes to almost every morning of his life. Even the faint burning of the chlorine fumes in the back of his throat is good. It contains the promise of silent relief. In a few moments he will be gliding through the water, lost in his own private world.

But these are small pleasures; tiny joys invisible to the untrained eye. Simon doesn't pretend otherwise. The sights and smells of the pool are a momentary diversion from the morning routine.

Breakfast in silence. Twenty minutes in the car—more silence. His father hasn't talked to him much since he came home and told his parents he'd decided to become a Christian. But at least home is bearable. The swim team is insufferable.

"Hey Simon, saw you talking to Kate yesterday. Don't

get too close. You know the rules. No sex before marriage!"

"Yeah, what would Jesus do?"

"He wouldn't know what to do!" (Laughter.)

"Whatever you do, don't look at her in her swim suit!"

The jokes change every morning in the way that only teenage boys exploring their limited creativity can manage, but the subject matter never varies. Thankfully the whistle interrupts and the derision is drowned by the demands of the morning's training. Simon dives into liquid bliss—an hour alone with God to pray and to plead for strength to keep serving Christ. An hour to wonder why he ever decided to pursue this whole Christian thing at all...

SALLY WAKES WEARILY IN the morning darkness. At least, it is probably dark outside. But the hospital is never really dark. The muted lights never sleep; nor do the machines with their constant hum. In her better moments she pretends they are married. She imagines the lights declaring their undying love for the hum and the hum promising never to leave, in sickness or in health. But it is a strange marriage—they **never** leave each other's side.

Unfortunately, Sally's better moments have been playing hide-and-seek for weeks now. At first they weren't very good at it. She could find them when she needed to—when visitors came and stood gravely by the bed, or when Jane dropped in to keep her up to date with what was happening at school. But since Friday, something has changed. Her better moments are getting smarter, more elusive. It's getting harder to look on the bright side as the morphine battles to keep the pain at bay.

The pain. It had been quite innocuous at first. "Growing pains", her mum had said, before they knew better. And in a way, she was right. Something is growing and the pain and the growing are related. But it is another unnatural marriage. This one will give birth to death and not life.

It isn't fair. Everyone says so. She is only 17.

Sally gets sick of the clichés, but she also understands that sometimes hopelessly inadequate words are better than no words at all. She needs words—words to give expression to the anger and disappointment. She wants to meet God face to face and ask her questions. She wants to make him give her some answers.

Yet, for all of the anger and disappointment, in her frustration and grief her trust does not diminish. God's Spirit is powerful.

She knows that her Father, who once spoke life into existence out of nothing, can mould life out of something as inconsequential as death. She knows his commitment to her. She reminds herself each day of the one great truth: God so loved the world that he gave his only begotten Son. And she reads and re-reads the Bible her grandmother gave her, until the pages are worn. Not that she needs the pages any more. She knows her favourite verse by heart: "He will wipe away every tear from their eyes, and death shall be no more, neither shall there be mourning, nor crying, nor pain any more, for the former things have passed away" (Rev 21:4).

In God's timing, Sally will be born into her heavenly home before her 18th birthday in this world.

God is very faithful.

It's not surprising that a book about suffering begins with stories of suffering—and with good reason. Suffering is not really a philosophical problem. Suffering is experienced, not just contemplated; it's often an event in our guts before it's a problem in our heads.

But I have told—in fact, made up—these particular stories for a reason. Let me ask you an uncomfortable question. If an angel appeared to you tonight in a dream and said that you had to choose between experiencing either Simon's suffering or Sally's suffering, which would you choose and why?

I know what my answer would be. I would choose Simon's any day. It involves less physical pain, it seems shorter term and, most importantly of all, Simon will still be alive in a year from now. By just about any sensible measure, Sally's suffering is more significant. It's a no-brainer. If I had to choose, I would choose Simon's suffering.

But stop with me for a moment and reflect on how I made my decision. Being alive rather than dead in a year's time is a big deal for me. But what would God's word say (if I took the time to look)? When the apostle Paul says, "to live is Christ, and to die is gain" (Phil 1:21), what sort of priorities does that reflect? If being dead in a year's time means being face to face with my Lord in glory, is it really so bad after all?

And what about Paul's other statement just one verse earlier?

> It is my eager expectation and hope that I will not
> be at all ashamed, but that with full courage now as
> always Christ will be honoured in my body, whether
> by life or by death. (Phil 1:20)

If the most important thing in the world is to cling to Christ and to honour him, who is in the gravest danger? Sally's faith, although tested, never waivers while Simon questions deeply. Who will still belong to Jesus in one year's time?

So let me ask you again: which form of suffering would you choose, and why?

It's a potentially foolish question. Comparing our sufferings in order to decide whose suffering is worse is a ridiculous exercise. I've heard many immature Christians arguing about why their life is harder and more painful than everyone else's. Usually the argument is dreadfully self-centred and vacuous, not to mention worse than watching paint dry for the onlookers. It's a foolish conversation that leads nowhere.

Yet sometimes comparisons are invaluable. When I used to talk to my wife's grandmother about what her childhood was like, hearing her stories helped me and my children to understand how much we are products of our own times. My kids could hardly believe that people used to walk miles to and from school every day as well as doing chores that my kids would consider slave labour. But it helped them to think about themselves and their own experiences. My grandmother (in-law) didn't live in a draconian society that robbed people of their choices and their youth. She just grew up in a relatively loving family who did their best to care for each other with what God had given them.

The point of the Simon and Sally stories is not to invent some scale of Christian suffering. We don't need to compare our own level of martyrdom with those around us, or start our own reality TV contest—*World's Most Persevering Christian*. The point is rather to raise some important questions about suffering. What sorts of values and ideals do we have about suffering? What is our theology of suffering? And does it match up with what the Bible really has to say about suffering?

That last question is really the central question of this book—a book that occurred more by accident than design. I didn't set out to write a book; I set out to produce a set of Bible studies about suffering. And as I began, I thought I knew pretty much what I was going to say. But the more I read the Bible, trying to find the right passages to make the points I thought I needed to make, the more uneasy I felt. It became obvious to me that my ideas about suffering hadn't been sufficiently shaped by God's word.

John Wesley has been famously quoted as saying, "Our people die well". It's a sentiment worth repeating. How should we live as God's people in the face of suffering? What does it mean to suffer—and even die—well?

That's what this book is all about. It's not a theodicy (an explanation of how God is all good and all powerful and yet we still live in a world of suffering). And it's not a set of stories written by those who have suffered. Rather, it is a biblical exploration of what God wants us to know about him and about our world when it comes to suffering. It is an encouragement to do what the Bible calls on us to do: to be people who suffer well.

I am persuaded that the key to suffering well lies in understanding the fullness of God's revelation about suffering. Almost ironically, this means we won't find God's true comfort unless we wrestle with ideas that are initially confronting and even painful. And so a large part of what follows is a challenge simply to hear and accept God's view of suffering. We live in a world that refuses to look to God's truth for comfort, and we are affected by our world, so the pages of this book may be as disquieting as they are encouraging. I make no apology for that. I believe that God's unsettling truth is much better for us than pillow-soft platitudes.

In other words, this book is more of an inoculation than a remedy. Its aim is to help us arm ourselves with the truth so that we're equipped to suffer well when the time comes.

Nevertheless, I know from my own experience that some will find their way here in the midst of great pain. Whether you are currently suffering greatly or only a little, I would encourage you to read what follows prayerfully, with your Bible open, asking God to help you see the world through his eyes. In the depths of God's riches are truths about suffering that are treasures beyond compare, if you are willing to see them.

However, before we get to God's word, there is something we need to do first. Sometimes, in order to hear the truth, we need to remove the earplugs that keep us from listening properly. All of us have had the experience at some time or another of speaking to someone who doesn't listen to us because they have already made up their mind about what we are saying—and we can be guilty of this ourselves. So often we pretend to listen to others, but all we hear are the stories in our own head. We are in grave danger of doing the same thing when it comes to hearing God's word about suffering.

We've lost touch with biblical truth because of the constant hum of worldly thinking that swirls around in our heads. The first question we need to ask is this: when it comes to suffering, are we prisoners of our age, or slaves to biblical truth?

Chapter 2

THE STORIES IN OUR HEADS

PEOPLE LOVE STORIES. THE best television shows tell a gripping story in each episode as well as over the course of an entire series. But you don't need million-dollar budgets to tell a good story. Well-written children's stories can be just as intriguing. We invited a young couple to our house for dinner last year, and I remember how they sat and listened to our children's story time, totally rapt. Stories have the power to shape our minds and change our hearts.

Sometimes our stories are tales of adventure and adversity.

"Do you remember that day we went hiking in the forest? The rain absolutely poured down and the leeches slurped out of the ground."

"Yeah! By the end of the day they were latching onto us faster than we could pull them off."

"Do you remember Dad's shirt in the car on the way home—that big blood splotch we found on his back? That was the biggest, fattest leech I've ever seen!"

Stories like this help us to laugh together and share the pain of difficulty. But stories can do more than that. We often tell stories to inform. Societies tell stories to explain the way the world is and to teach people how it should be.

In this chapter, I want to draw attention to three stories that are so common, so widespread and so deeply embedded in Western culture that most of us take them entirely for granted. But these stories profoundly shape how we think about the world, and in particular how we think about suffering.

Story 1: Humans must be free

One of the most powerful cultural stories of our age is the story of intellectual freedom. It's been told so often in the last century or so that it has become part of the fabric of Western cultural life. Let me show you just one example of it.

In the 1980s, a famous scientist called Carl Sagan produced a documentary series called *Cosmos*. It was seen more than 500 million people worldwide, and a book to accompany the series was published. In it, Sagan explained life in our modern world. Speaking of the discovery that the Earth revolves around the sun, he wrote:

> The epochal confrontation between the two views
> of the Cosmos—Earth-centred and Sun-centred—

SUFFERING WELL

reached a climax in the sixteenth and seventeenth centuries in the person of a man who was, like Ptolemy, both astrologer and astronomer. He lived in a time when the human spirit was fettered and the mind chained; when the ecclesiastical pronouncements of a millennium or two earlier on scientific matters were considered more reliable than contemporary findings made with techniques unavailable to the ancients; when deviations, even on arcane theological matters, from the prevailing doxological preferences, Catholic or Protestant, were punished by humiliation, taxation, exile, torture or death. The heavens were inhabited by angels, demons and the Hand of God, turning the planetary crystal spheres. Science was barren of the idea that underlying the phenomena of Nature might be the laws of physics. But the brave and lonely struggle of this man was to ignite the modern scientific revolution.[1]

Sagan was speaking about Johannes Kepler. But the story is the story of our age. It is the story that explains how we have been freed from religion by those who were unwilling to be bound by superstition. In a world where religion and darkness reigned, some people didn't listen to what they were told and instead just examined the evidence. Our world, once imprisoned by ignorance and fear, has been liberated by the bravery of those willing to stand up against intolerant ideology. Dogged pursuit of

---

1   C Sagan, *Cosmos*, Random House, New York, 1980, p. 41.

the truth has won for us a wonderful new world full of freedom.

At the heart of this story lies the idea that true human freedom comes from rejecting God and exploring the world on our own terms. It's not a new story. You'll find it on the pages of your daily newspaper and on the virtual pages of bloggers all over the world. And of course we've all heard the earliest form of this story—the story of Adam and Eve in Genesis 3.

The reason for telling the story here is that the story of human intellectual freedom is also the modern story of suffering.

Story 2: Suffering and the new morality

The second big story of our modern world that I want to draw your attention to is the story of individual morality. Now that humanity has cast off the superstitions of believing in God and (supposedly) found true freedom, morality has become largely relative. That is, there is now no 'God' up there telling us what to do, and making pronouncements about moral absolutes. There is no divine law dictating what is right and wrong for everyone. Each of us can now decide for ourselves what is right and what is wrong.

One of the worst things you can do in our society is to try to impose your morality on someone else. Who are you to tell me how I should express my sexuality? Who are you to make rules about whether women should be allowed to abort their babies? Who are you to deny people the right to end their lives with dignity if they should so choose?

The modern story of human freedom is also the story of moral relativism: there is no absolute right and wrong, just different versions of morality that we each choose for ourselves.

But there is a twist to this new morality that has arisen out of our modern quest for freedom. For, while the atheistic worldview says that everybody should be free to do whatever they like, some things are still universally seen as evil. The genocides of the last century cannot be condoned, on any worldview. And despite attempts to promote some level of acceptance for paedophilia, there is still, thankfully, an almost total condemnation of the practice.

So if there is no outside authority or 'God' to declare that some things are always evil (like racism or genocide), on what basis can we make moral arguments? How can we declare some things to be really wrong and immoral?

The answer our society has come up with is based on the avoidance of pain and suffering. If something causes suffering, then it is wrong—almost by definition— and other considerations must take second place. For example, modern humanistic atheists would argue that homosexuality must be legitimised and celebrated because to say that it is sinful or illegal causes suffering for homosexual people. They have the right to be happy and to avoid the suffering that comes from people questioning their lifestyle choices. They also have the right to avoid the suffering that comes from being unable to freely and genuinely express their sexuality.

Likewise, our society argues that women have suffered deeply over the centuries for bearing the burden of procreation and childrearing. For women to be free of suffering they need to have the option of abortion—especially where the child might be born with a disability that would lead to great effort and heartache in caring for a child who may never speak or show affection. Similar logic also applies to the euthanasia argument. We kill dogs when they are in pain—surely human beings should be allowed the same dignity.

These are important issues that deserve a detailed biblical response, but that is not our task here. What we need to see is that each of these arguments assumes that suffering is always an evil that must be avoided. In a world without God, painlessness is the new moral standard. The only great truth is that suffering must be avoided at all costs.

What is the story of modern life? People should be free to do whatever they like, as long as they don't **hurt** anyone else in the process.

Story 3: Suffering and the death of God

The third story follows on from the first two, and reinforces both. It is the story of the death of God. And it starts with a question: if the avoidance of suffering is now our basis for morality, then how can we believe in a God who allows suffering?

Sir David Attenborough, renowned naturalist and BBC documentary maker, is often asked in letters from viewers why he doesn't give credit to God for the wonders of the creation that he spends so much time filming and studying. His answer goes like this:

> "They always mean beautiful things like hummingbirds.
> I always reply by saying that I think of a little child in
> east Africa with a worm burrowing through his eyeball.
> The worm cannot live in any other way, except by
> burrowing through eyeballs. I find that hard to reconcile
> with the notion of a divine and benevolent creator."[2]

For many people, suffering is a major part of the argument against God's existence. The very presence of suffering in our world, not to mention its breadth and depth, is a key piece of evidence. If we really have an all-good and all-powerful God then how can there possibly be such suffering?

You only need to think about the past century to understand the emotional power of this point. The 'war to end all wars' was followed barely two decades later by an even more bloody conflict. Pol Pot's Cambodia, Stalin's Soviet Union, and more recently the atrocities in Rwanda and Chechnya have given us examples of suffering that boggle the mind. But this human-inflicted suffering almost pales into insignificance beside events like the Spanish flu pandemic in 1918, or the great Chinese famine (1959-1961) in which something like 30 million

---

2   R Butt, 'Attenborough reveals creationist hate mail for not crediting God', *The Guardian*, 27 January 2009, available online (viewed 8 August 2011): www.guardian.co.uk/world/2009/jan/27/david-attenborough-science

people starved to death. The 2004 tsunami in the Indian Ocean was almost a nothing in comparison. Yet watching and hearing about the deaths of almost a quarter of a million people rocked our world. How can anyone believe in a loving God in a world that is so broken?

Alongside this argument—that suffering means there is no God—is another important argument widely accepted in our world: that religion is the greatest cause of human suffering. The so-called New Atheists have made worldwide reputations, and not a little money for their cause, by exploiting this widely held belief. On the publisher's website for Dawkins's *The God Delusion*, we read:

> Dawkins makes a compelling case that belief in God is not just irrational but incredibly harmful. In the past five years, we have witnessed the evils that men do in the name of God. Still, many religious people find it hard to imagine how, without religion, one can be good. Dawkins argues that our moral sense has a Darwinian origin, and he answers, "Do you really mean to tell me the only reason you try to be good is to gain God's approval and reward or to avoid his disapproval and punishment? That's not morality, that's just sucking up." Further, and more seriously, Dawkins says, "Those who literally wish to base their morality on the Bible have either not read it or have not understood it".[3]

---

3   Houghton Mifflin Harcourt, New York, 2011 (viewed 12 August 2011): www.houghtonmifflinbooks.com/booksellers/press_release/delusion/

Comedians Penn and Teller are quoted on the same site:

> "*The God Delusion* is smart, compassionate, and true,
> like ice, like fire. If this book doesn't change the world,
> we're all screwed."[4]

The point could not be clearer: the only possible end to human-induced suffering is to reject religion, and believe in science and reason alone.

And so the circle is complete. For if the avoidance of suffering is the foundation for morality, what does that mean for the God who made our world? Given all the suffering in this world, he must either be cruel or not exist. If God made us and then placed us in a world where we suffer, he is acting like a young boy pulling the wings off flies for fun. Richard Dawkins, among others, does not hold back in ramming home his conclusion:

> The God of the Old Testament is arguably the most
> unpleasant character in all fiction: jealous and proud
> of it; a petty, unjust, unforgiving control-freak; a
> vindictive, bloodthirsty ethnic cleanser; a misogynistic,
> homophobic, racist, infanticidal, genocidal, filicidal,
> pestilential, megalomaniacal, sadomasochistic,
> capriciously malevolent bully.[5]

Ethics in a godless world is grounded in stories about

---

4   Houghton Mifflin Harcourt, New York, 2011 (viewed 12 August 2011):
     www.houghtonmifflinbooks.com/booksellers/press_release/delusion/
5   R Dawkins, *The God Delusion*, Mariner Books, New York, 2008, p. 51.

suffering and the evils of God. Whether or not our neighbours would put it as bluntly and angrily as Richard Dawkins, it is impossible to avoid the questions of our friends and family. I constantly meet people from all walks of life who make many of these objections to the Christian faith, without ever having read or even heard of Richard Dawkins (or Christopher Hitchens or Sam Harris). The reason is that these men—who in many ways are the storytellers of our age—are actually just retelling a story that has been passed down from one generation to the next for several centuries now. These stories have been part of our cultural memory since at least the 1700s (thanks to David Hume). But for the first time in history, they are beginning to become the dominant cultural memory.

In our brave new world, suffering means that God is immoral and that Christians are immoral. Our only hope is a world freed from the Christian God, in which humanity invents its own understanding of right and wrong, guided by reason alone.

How should Christians respond?

How should we respond to these stories? My instant response is to rush headlong into answering them. I want to point out, for example, that atheism is not the only logical response to suffering—far from it.

Our age is not the only age to experience terrible tragedy. Between 1346 and 1351, the Black Plague is estimated to have killed about 100 million people, or approximately 50 per cent of the European population. The Justinian plague in the middle of the 6th century killed almost as many.[6] For as long as humanity has existed, we have known of the possibility of death on a grand scale.

How did those who lived through these tragedies cope with their suffering? None of the literature from those periods suggests that people leaped to atheism as a philosophical response to their suffering. Indeed, quite a bit of evidence from the time of the Black Plague points to a widespread understanding of the plague as an act of God's wrath and as a sign of humanity's guilt.

Clearly then, our understanding of suffering comes not just from the experience itself. As in all things, our views are also shaped by **how the culture around us makes sense of suffering**. And this is our real problem when it comes to knowing God's truth.

The modern story of suffering and the evil of God has become the foundational story of our age. What is the result? The most significant result is that we have begun reading our Bibles in light of these stories rather than reading these stories in light of the Bible. The stories in our heads—the stories our culture teaches from birth—teach us that humans should be free at all costs; that suffering is the greatest evil; that avoiding suffering is the basis for morality; and that therefore suffering is a

---

6   All of these figures come from two Wikipedia articles (viewed 12 August 2011): www.en.wikipedia.org/wiki/Justinian_plague and www.en.wikipedia.org/wiki/Black_plague

big obstacle for belief in God and for Christian faith. And as we come to the Scriptures, we can't help but filter them through this grid.

Where do we see this in practice? Well, it's there in our treatment of the Old Testament. Christians are tearing the pages of the Old Testament out of their Bibles—not physically, but virtually. The Old Testament is still in our Bibles; we just don't read it. Our heads are so full of the world's stories, we are afraid that reading Deuteronomy or Joshua or Ezekiel might lead to us giving up the faith. How can we defend God's commands to his people to wipe out the nations before them as they entered the Promised Land?

But it is not just our treatment of the Old Testament that suffers. Even when we come across words about hell and judgement in the New Testament, we spend most of our time trying to excuse God. Pastors spend whole sermons giving a theodicy (an explanation of how God can be good and still allow suffering in the world) without calling on people to respond in repentance before the righteous judge of the world. When suffering comes up in the Bible, we often find ourselves questioning God rather than asking ourselves the hard questions.

This 'modern anti-suffering grid' also affects the way we respond to natural disasters. We cannot imagine an all-powerful God who would allow such disasters to occur, let alone **cause** them to occur. It has become commonplace to hear sound bites in the media of Christian religious leaders responding to these kinds of events. Often they are saying things like "God had nothing to do with this earthquake" or "God was totally absent from this tsunami". When pressed, these same religious leaders will often confess to having no idea about what God was doing at all.

I am not pretending that suffering does not raise big questions about God's character. Indeed, it does. Nor am I saying that we should always avoid these questions. But I am convinced that our world's thinking has so affected us that we are in great danger of missing some of the central truths of God's revelation.

The rest of this book is therefore an attempt to think from the **Bible's** perspective about the nature of suffering. We will only truly understand God's world when we see its suffering through his eyes. And we will only be thoroughly equipped to live faithfully in the face of suffering when we see the world through God's eyes. As we remove the blinkers we've inherited from our world, we may even see what we are afraid to see—that suffering is essential for those who follow Jesus, and that only those who follow Jesus will learn to suffer well.

Chapter 3

WHAT QUESTIONS SHOULD WE ASK?

I LEARNED MANY LESSONS growing up in the 1980s. Spiral perms really were a one-off sensation; fluorescent pink can only last for so long as a fashion statement; you need a minimum of 12-inch thick concrete if you want to build a nuclear fallout shelter... But I digress. The lesson that concerns us here is the importance of what we say.

The 1980s was a time of prominence for the feminist movement. Many significant social changes came about as the feminists campaigned to change our use of language. I remember our school teachers drumming into us the importance of non-sexist language. We could no longer talk about 'the chairman of the board'; it had to be 'the chairperson'. The policeman at the corner needed to be known as a 'law enforcement officer'. 'Mankind', ironically, became 'hu-man-ity' (I guess hu-person was rather clumsy).

Every time we went to write 'he', we were forced to stop and ask: should we use 'he', 'she' or 'it'? Feminism changed our thinking about gender by causing us to ask its questions over and over again. Feminism also taught us that the way we speak and write shapes, as well as reflects, what we think of as important.

What does this mean for our topic of suffering? If we find ourselves asking the question "Can a good God allow such a messed up world?" every time we read the Old Testament or watch the news, then it is highly likely that our thinking is already being changed. We are already asking the world's questions and adopting our society's worldview. What we need to do is look at how the Bible responds to the issues of suffering. We need to begin with God's response to the kinds of questions our world asks about suffering.

The issue of God's justice in a broken world is raised a number of times in the Bible. And as far as I can see, on each occasion the question is answered in a way that is entirely foreign to us. Let's have a look at three different places where the Bible addresses the question of God's justice in a broken world: the confounding case of Job, the cry of Habakkuk, and Paul's argument with the Jews in Rome.

Job

Perhaps the most curious case of all is the case of Job. Job is introduced as an almost superhumanly good guy:

> There was a man in the land of Uz whose name was
> Job, and that man was blameless and upright, one
> who feared God and turned away from evil. (Job 1:1)

What more could be said to make the point? Only Jesus himself was more righteous than this! But it is no accident Job is introduced to us in this way. We are supposed to see that Job is a deeply pious, God-fearing man. This is what makes his suffering so much worse.

Unbeknownst to Job, even as he offers extra burnt offerings for each of his children, Satan enters into the presence of God to question Job's loyalty. Is Job only righteous because God has looked after him so well? Would Job reject God if life was a little more uncomfortable?

God gives Satan permission to find the answer. So Satan takes away Job's property, his children, and his health, leaving him a broken man. The rest of the book of Job is an extended meditation on what to make of all of this. What does Job's suffering mean for Job? What does Job's suffering mean for God?

The first part of the book (chapters 3-31) records a number of conversations, or even arguments, between Job and his three friends, Eliphaz, Bildad and Zophar. These men are certain Job has done something wrong. After all, conventional wisdom demands that a man who has suffered as much as Job must have sinned. Bildad provides an excellent example of this kind of argument in chapter 8. He says that God is always right, always pure and just. Therefore, if Job's children have died, then it must be because they did something wrong (Job 8:1-4). God has rightly dealt with them according to their transgressions. And if that is the case with Job's children, then it must also be the case with Job.

But the reader knows from the very beginning that this is not the case. And Job, although he knows nothing of Satan's heavenly conversation with God, knows he has done no wrong. But this leaves Job with somewhat of a dilemma. On the one hand, Job knows that God is perfect and pure and righteous. He says:

> "With God are wisdom and might;
>> he has counsel and understanding.
> If he tears down, none can rebuild;
>> if he shuts a man in, none can open.
> If he withholds the waters, they dry up;
>> if he sends them out, they overwhelm the land.
> With him are strength and sound wisdom;
>> the deceived and the deceiver are his." (Job 12:13-16)

On the other hand, Job also knows that his situation is not right. So much so that Job is bold enough to call on God for a face-to-face meeting:

> "But I would speak to the Almighty,
>> and I desire to argue my case with God...
> Let me have silence, and I will speak,
>> and let come on me what may.
> Why should I take my flesh in my teeth
>> and put my life in my hand?
> Though he slay me, I will hope in him;
>> yet I will argue my ways to his face." (Job 13:3, 13-15)

What is the result of Job's cry? In the second half of the book, Job gets his meeting with God. God says to Job:

> "Who is this that darkens counsel by words without
>   knowledge?
> Dress for action like a man;
>   I will question you, and you make it known to me.
> Where were you when I laid the foundation of the
>   earth?
>   Tell me, if you have understanding." (Job 38:2-4)

What follows is God's declaration of his character to Job. He reminds Job that he alone is the creator of the world and that he alone is the powerful ruler over all Job sees. After meeting God face to face, all Job can say is this:

> "I know that you can do all things,
>   and that no purpose of yours can be thwarted.
> 'Who is this that hides counsel without knowledge?'
> Therefore I have uttered what I did not understand,
>   things too wonderful for me, which I did not know.
> 'Hear, and I will speak;
>   I will question you, and you make it known to me.'
> I had heard of you by the hearing of the ear,
>   but now my eye sees you;
> therefore I despise myself,
>   and repent in dust and ashes." (Job 42:2-6)

Job encounters God face to face. He meets the all-powerful creator and ruler of the world, and all he can do is fall on his knees and worship God. Job never finds out what happened in heaven. He never finds out the reason for his suffering. He never has his questions answered.

He simply meets God, and all of his issues dissolve. There is nothing he can do before the face of the Lord except to grant him honour.

The point of the book of Job is not to explain the reason for every episode of suffering in the lives of innocent people. It is to remind us that God has reasons beyond our reasons, and to call us to humbly rely on him. Job suffered deeply. But God taught him that he didn't need all of his questions answered; he just needed to know the living God.

As Job suffers and meets God, we are reminded of a number of crucial biblical presuppositions that run entirely counter to everything the world would have us believe. Not only is suffering not a reason to doubt God, but Job also remains steadfast in his belief that every aspect of suffering is in God's hands. From his response to his unhelpful wife ("Shall we receive good from God, and shall we not receive evil?" in 2:10) through to his extended meditations ("If he tears down, none can rebuild; if he shuts a man in, none can open" in 12:14) Job reveals his wisdom. Job knows that God is the sovereign Lord in control of all things—so he must also be sovereign over suffering.

Furthermore, Job reminds us that the solution to our suffering will be found not in receiving answers to all our questions but in seeing God himself. As much as Job wishes to question God, the reality is that it is God who will question Job—just as he will question each and every one of us in judgement. This is a theme to which we must return, but first let's consider Habakkuk.

SUFFERING WELL

Habakkuk

We don't know much about the exact circumstances or timing of Habakkuk's prophecy. But his questions are universal questions. Habakkuk lives amongst the people of Judah, and as he looks around at his countrymen— those who are supposed to love and worship Yahweh— he finds only dishonesty and disobedience. Habakkuk despairs because he sees injustice and feels that God does nothing about it. How can these evil people get away with their evil?

> O LORD, how long shall I cry for help,
>   and you will not hear?
> Or cry to you "Violence!"
>   and you will not save?
> Why do you make me see iniquity,
>   and why do you idly look at wrong?
> Destruction and violence are before me;
>   strife and contention arise.
> So the law is paralysed,
>   and justice never goes forth.
> For the wicked surround the righteous;
>   so justice goes forth perverted. (Hab 1:2-4)

From our perspective, it is not a great leap from Habakkuk's question to the very question of God's existence. If the world is full of such great injustice and God never seems to do anything about it, is this because God is unjust or because God is not there? But Habakkuk will have none of that. He knows what God is like and he cries out to God for justice.

What is God's answer?

God's answer to Habakkuk is profoundly uncomfortable. God promises Habakkuk that he will use the Chaldeans, a "bitter and hasty nation" (1:6), to bring justice against his own people. The Chaldeans will come and Israel will be crushed and broken. God is going to use the injustice of one nation as judgement upon the injustice of another.

Habakkuk is understandably bewildered. God's apparent inactivity in the face of wrongdoing was nothing in comparison to this solution. Habakkuk cannot contain himself. "But God," he says, "if you give the Chaldeans the power to destroy nations, will their merciless killing ever come to an end?"[7] Habakkuk thinks perhaps the solution is worse than the problem.

God's answer is that he will also bring judgement on Chaldea, but in his own good time. Habakkuk will just have to wait until God is ready.

Apparently he learns his lesson because by the end of the book, Habakkuk declares:

> ...I will quietly wait for the day of trouble
>   to come upon people who invade us.
> Though the fig tree should not blossom,
>   nor fruit be on the vines,
> the produce of the olive fail

---

7   This is my somewhat loose paraphrase! If you want to read exactly what Habakkuk says, you can find it in Habakkuk 1:12-17.

and the fields yield no food,
the flock be cut off from the fold
and there be no herd in the stalls,
yet I will rejoice in the LORD;
I will take joy in the God of my salvation.
GOD, the Lord, is my strength;
he makes my feet like the deer's;
he makes me tread on my high places. (Hab 3:16-19)

Although the circumstances are different, and although Habakkuk does not meet God face to face in the way Job does, the fundamental truths about God and his world are the same. Again, God is the one in complete control. Chaldea can only come against Israel because God has determined it to be so. But, incredibly, even as they attack Israel under God's sovereign hand, they also attack Israel in their own arrogance and wickedness. And so God prepares their judgement even as he uses their wickedness as the instrument of his righteousness. The world experiences suffering not because God is **out** of control but because God is **in** control. And the solution to suffering is not to see everything sorted out in our time, but to wait patiently for God to act according to his character.

Let's see one more example.

Paul and the Roman Jews

Our third example appears, at least at first glance, to be a slightly strange one. In the apostle Paul's letter to the Romans, he goes to great lengths to explain the nature of his message about Jesus. And in the course of explaining God's righteousness revealed in Jesus, he spends considerable time explaining the nature of God's judgement—his judgement on the Gentile world (1:18-32), and his judgement on those who would call themselves God's people (chapter 2). At the end of Paul's long explanation about Israel's failure to honour the God who gave them his law, the obvious question becomes "Then what advantage has the Jew? Or what is the value of circumcision?" (3:1).

Paul responds to this question by reminding us that the Jews were entrusted with the oracles of God. It is no small thing to have the very words of the creator! The Jews were greatly blessed as God's chosen people.

At this point we need to slow down a little, because Paul's argument in chapter 3 is quite dense.

God was gracious to Israel, but she was not faithful to God. She took God's words and disobeyed them (assuming that just being God's chosen people would be enough to make her right with God). But, and this is Paul's main point, the Jews' faithlessness does not nullify God's faithfulness. Whatever the Jews might have done, God is still faithful to his promises. This raises the obvious (and for our discussion, incredibly important) objection: "But if our unrighteousness serves to show the righteousness of God, what shall we say? That God is unrighteous to inflict wrath on us?" (3:5).

It seems (and we will come to this in more detail when we look at Romans 9 shortly) that God planned the Jewish rejection of his truth **so that** he could display his righteousness to the whole world. But if this is true, then the Jews could rightly argue that their rejection of God wasn't their fault. If God is in charge, and the Jews sinned, then God is responsible—right? And this means that, in their own words, "God is unrighteous to inflict wrath on us". If the Jewish disobedience to God's truth was part of God's plan, then surely God shouldn't judge them for it!

You can't really fault their logic. But that's what makes Paul's answer so puzzling. Is God unrighteous to inflict wrath on the Jews? "By no means! For then how could God judge the world?" (3:6). It doesn't seem like an argument so much as a statement. We want Paul to prove to us that God is righteous and therefore equipped to judge. But Paul responds in reverse: because God will judge the world, we know that he is righteous. The absolute bedrock truth for Paul is that the God who made the world can judge it. God is the righteous creator and ruler of the world—so when you see Israel being judged, the one sure conclusion is that the problem lies with Israel and not with God.

Paul's argument is grounded on a profound biblical truth: God is God and we are not. God is the sovereign Lord; the creator of everything that is, seen and unseen; the ruler over the past, the present and the future. We are his creatures, made by him for his purposes.

Paul reaches the same conclusion when the issue of God's righteousness comes up again in Romans 9-11. Paul spends much of Romans 3-8 explaining how Jesus' death and resurrection deals perfectly with human sin and brings us permanent hope for the future. But of course the certainty of God's love and grace can be held up to question if God has proved to be unfaithful in the past. If God promised Israel that they were his people and then rejected them, can we trust him now when he says Jesus has forgiven all our sins and brought us hope for the future?

This is the issue Paul takes up in Romans 9. Having declared so wonderfully and boldly at the end of Romans 8 that not even death itself can separate us from God's love in Christ, Paul comes to the question: then what about God's promises to the Jews? On the one hand, the nation of Israel is the people of God. As Paul puts it, "to them belong the adoption, the glory, the covenants, the giving of the law, the worship, and the promises" (9:4). They seem to have everything. And yet, when Jesus came, they rejected the Messiah, God's king, the one they were waiting for. What happened?

Without going into too much detail, Paul's answer is that God planned for the Jews to reject Jesus so that the gospel might go to the nations and through the nations back to Israel. God's plan was that everyone, Jew and Gentile alike, would come to salvation through faith in Jesus. And so God planned that Jew and Gentile alike would be under sin and that Israel as a nation would reject the Messiah when he came.

As Paul explains all of this, he shows us how completely God is in control of human history. He does it by relating two situations from Israel's history. The first involves Isaac's twin sons, Jacob and Esau. Before

Esau and Jacob were even born, God had chosen one of them to receive the promise. The older one would serve the younger one because God decided it would be so. Hundreds of years later, with Israel living in captivity in Egypt, God chose to harden Pharaoh's heart in order to display his power by rescuing his people. Both inside and outside of Israel, God worked in history to reveal his own glory. And Paul's conclusion couldn't be clearer: "So then [God] has mercy on whomever he wills, and he hardens whomever he wills" (9:18).

God is in control. God chose Jacob as his. God hardened Pharaoh's heart. What is the obvious response? Paul knows only too well how we are likely to respond: "You will say to me then, 'Why does he still find fault? For who can resist his will?'" (9:19). It is basically the same objection that was raised back in chapter 3. If God is in charge of everything and God causes people to be hardened, then surely they are not personally responsible for their hardening? Of course God can't hold them accountable!

But, according to Scripture, he can. How does Paul put it?

> But who are you, O man, to answer back to God? Will what is moulded say to its moulder, "Why have you made me like this?" Has the potter no right over the clay, to make out of the same lump one vessel for honourable use and another for dishonourable use?
> (Rom 9:20-21)

Paul is not being original here; he is reusing a prophetic

Old Testament image. Isaiah and Jeremiah used the image of the potter and the clay to describe our relationship with God. Each time the meaning is the same. In the beginning at the dawn of time, God moulded a man, Adam, from the dust of the earth. God took what was lifeless and breathed life into our frail frames. And the creature formed from the dust of the ground—the creature of clay—is in no position to speak back to God or to demand answers from him.

Pharaoh and all Egypt suffered terribly under the plagues. God was responsible. But the clay's response should have been, "God is the creator and he can do what he likes with his creation".

Jacob was chosen before he was born to inherit the promise, and Esau was not. Yet the dust cannot accuse God. Esau cannot claim that God is unfair.

All through the Bible we are given picture after picture of God's complete control of his creation, which means the suffering of God's creation occurs by his hands. Hear these words from the Bible:

"I form light and create darkness,
    I make well-being and create calamity,
I am the LORD, who does all these things." (Isa 45:7)

"Does disaster come to a city,
    unless the LORD has done it?" (Amos 3:6)

Is it not from the mouth of the Most High
    that good and bad come? (Lam 3:38)

"With God are wisdom and might;
　　he has counsel and understanding.
If he tears down, none can rebuild;
　　if he shuts a man in, none can open...
He makes nations great, and he destroys them;
　　he enlarges nations, and leads them away."

(Job 12:13-14, 23)

Scripture never suggests suffering and difficulty come because God is out of control; rather, Scripture suggests they come because he is **in** control. Everything comes from his hand.

So what do we make of it all?

If you are anything like me, you may feel shocked at this point. Even if you have seen these passages before, you may still feel slightly unsettled. Why is the world like this? Why has God done it this way? These are not questions that will go away easily. I have a good friend who is slowly wasting away from muscular dystrophy. He is one of the godliest and most cheerful men I know. How can God do this? I have friends who lost a baby at 36 weeks of pregnancy. Why did God allow that to happen? These questions are deep and they are personal. They are questions that cry out for an answer.

But even as we acknowledge the significance of our own questions, we need to remember to begin where God begins. Before we come to our questions, we must stop and hear God's questions. Our world wants us to look at the suffering of this fallen creation and ask the question, "Does God really exist?" But the Scriptures stand in complete contrast. The Bible calls on us to look at God's world under suffering and declare, "The Lord who created everything is in control!" The obvious question ensues: what does this mean for us?

It means that we must be ready to meet our maker. This is a rather old-fashioned and quaint idea, isn't it? Are you ready to meet your maker? It almost sounds out of place in the 21st century. But down through the ages, it's the first question God's people have asked in the face of suffering. The Bible isn't confused or uncertain about why our world is suffering. It is very clear. The world is suffering because it stands under the heavy hand of God's judgement. Romans 8:20 tells us that this creation has been "subjected to futility" by God. This creation is not all it will one day be, because God has made it like this for a time. Romans 1:18 puts it even more starkly. Right now, the wrath of God is being revealed against all the ungodliness and unrighteousness of men who suppress the truth about their creator.

Ecclesiastes puts it slightly differently, but no less clearly, when it speaks about our world as bent or crooked: "Consider the work of God: who can make straight what he has made crooked?" (7:13). For the writer of Ecclesiastes, our world—marked by suffering and death—is a world that has been bent out of shape **by God**.

Again, while this may surprise us at first, it shouldn't. We have known it from the very opening pages of the Bible. God's word to Adam at the Fall stands over all of humanity:

"Because you have listened to the voice of your wife
    and have eaten of the tree
of which I commanded you,
    'You shall not eat of it,'
cursed is the ground because of you;
    in pain you shall eat of it all the days of your life;
thorns and thistles it shall bring forth for you;
    and you shall eat the plants of the field.
By the sweat of your face
    you shall eat bread,
till you return to the ground,
    for out of it you were taken;
for you are dust,
    and to dust you shall return." (Gen 3:17-19)

We live in a world marked by death and suffering because God has visited upon us the results of our sin. As we have rejected God and so rejected each other, God has given us a world in which we share the effects of our own sin and the sins of others. Suffering will always be a part of a fallen world in which God actively brings on us the fruit of our disobedience.

We mustn't misunderstand. This does not mean that each instance of suffering is directly related to the sinfulness of a particular individual. We've already seen in Job that there's still such thing as unmerited suffering, even in a rebellious world that stands under God's judgement. We are not to leap to the conclusion (as Job's friends did) that if someone suffers acutely, they must be notoriously sinful.

Yet the Bible also tells us as clearly as it can that we

are all sinful. We have all fallen short of the glory of God and we will all rightly face judgement, in this world and in the world to come.

This is why Jesus speaks so strongly and, to our ears at least, harshly about judgement. When some among the crowd tell Jesus about the way Pilate killed some Galileans and mixed their blood with the blood of their sacrifices, Jesus responded in an entirely unexpected way. Instead of calling down curses on Pilate, Jesus asked the crowd a question: "Do you think that these Galileans were worse sinners than all the other Galileans, because they suffered in this way? No, I tell you; but unless you repent, you will all likewise perish" (Luke 13:2-3). It is a response that would have shocked his listeners and which certainly shocks us. Jesus is not being warm and cuddly here, but brutally and lovingly honest.

Not all suffering is directly related to individual sinfulness, but we are all sinful and death will come to us all. Every single person will one day give an account before the God who made the world.

We began this chapter by seeing that the world wants us to respond to suffering by asking whether God exists. But the Bible has shown us that we should respond to suffering by recognizing the sovereign hand of the God who will one day judge the world. And this is why the gospel message is so offensive to people.

According to many of our friends and neighbours, human reason is the ultimate authority over everything. If God is there and he brings suffering, then he must explain himself. But God, who created us from the dust of the earth, says, "No!" He does not need to explain himself to us. **We** need to explain ourselves to **him**. This is not a comfortable truth, but it is vital that we begin with it if we are to truly understand suffering from God's perspective. We will never understand God's sovereign hand in suffering unless we understand that he is the creator and we are his creatures.

Chapter 4

BUT WHY?

"But why?" It's the perennial human question. Every three-year-old I've met asks it constantly. So it's not surprising that even as we read the Bible and see that God is in control of everything, there is still a part of us that longs to ask, "Why?" It was probably best captured for me by a man I know called Jacob.[8] Jacob was a Jewish man, studying for a PhD at the university where I work. For three years he came along, almost weekly, to our lunchtime campus Bible talks. We spoke at length about what it means to follow Jesus.

He was attracted to Christianity. He saw the lives of the people who were part of our group and he could see we were different. He was also intrigued by the fact that we took the Bible so seriously. But he always had

---

8   Not his real name.

questions. In some ways he had many questions, but in the end it really came down to one question: how can we possibly make sense of God's sovereignty and suffering?

After a series of Bible talks in Ezekiel, he came to me one day and said, "I understand what you are saying. I understand that God needs to be in control. I understand that God makes more sense of this world than anything else I have come across. But there's one thing I don't get. If I were to act like he acted—if I were to create people and then punish them for sins that I knew they were going to commit—then wouldn't I be a bully? How can you say that God is good and then say that he also judges people? If God was a heavenly bully rather than the good God that you say he is, how would he be any different?"

Jacob was a very perceptive man. He understood what the Bible was saying about God's sovereign control and he was asking a very important question. If God is really in control of everything, then how do we know he's really good? Couldn't he just say that good is evil and evil is good? Isn't he just like the schoolyard bully who has big enough biceps to persuade everyone else he is right?

We've already seen that we must be careful when asking questions of God. It is not something to be undertaken lightly. But Jacob's question is still an important one. Could it be that God is really evil?

To answer this question we need to investigate two wonderful truths about God. The first concerns the consistency of God's character. The Scriptures tell us that God is the same yesterday, today and forever. He isn't capricious. He isn't sweeter than honey one moment and then bitter as gall the next. He always acts in the same way, according to the constancy of his character.

James reminds us, "Every good gift and every perfect gift is from above, coming down from the Father of lights with whom there is no variation or shadow due to change" (Jas 1:17). God is good, and in his goodness he gives us all good things. But we must not misunderstand this. The constancy of God's character applies in all situations. Just as God is generous to all, and makes "his sun rise on the evil and on the good, and sends rain on the just and on the unjust" (Matt 5:45), so also he promises not to leave the guilty unpunished.

In the Old Testament, there is a vitally important event to which we must return over and over again if we are to understand God properly. It occurs at one of the most tragic moments in Israel's history, just after God delivers the Israelites from their oppression in Egypt.

Throughout the Old Testament, the exodus from Egypt is seen as the ultimate example of God's faithfulness and kindness towards Israel. God takes his people, who are living in captivity and working as slaves, and he rescues them from Pharaoh through mighty signs and wonders. God's people are protected while the Egyptians suffer. The Israelites leave Egypt with Egyptian gold and silver rattling in their pockets, and God keeps them safe as Pharaoh's army rages after them across the desert.

But the story doesn't end there. After crossing the Red Sea, the whole nation marches to the base of Mount Sinai and they gather together while Moses goes up on the mountain to speak with God. The problem is that Moses is gone for a rather long time—40 days to be precise. And the longer he is gone, the more anxious the people get. Is Moses really to be trusted? Is it comfortable here living on the edge of the desert? Finally, when the people can stand it no longer, they come to Aaron (Moses' brother) and plead: "Up, make us gods who shall go before us. As for this Moses, the man who brought us up out of the land of Egypt, we do not know what has become of him" (Exod 32:1).

What would you do if the people came to you? Aaron knows exactly what to do. He collects all their golden rings and earrings, melts them, and fashions a golden calf. The moment the people set their eyes on it, they cry out, "These are your gods, O Israel, who brought you up out of the land of Egypt!" (Exod 32:4). Having been rescued and protected by the Lord of the universe, the people of Israel promptly bow down and worship the work of their own hands. It is human folly at its worst; human folly we would all have been involved in, had we been there.

Back on the mountain, God responds righteously. He tells Moses he is going to consume the people in his wrath. Moses pleads with God to reconsider, although he is all too aware of the horror of Israel's rejection of God. Moses says later to Israel, "You have sinned a great sin. And now I will go up to the LORD; perhaps I can make atonement for your sin" (Exod 32:30).

What will God do to these people? How will he treat those whom he has rescued and made his own but who have so stupendously disobeyed him?

God does punish his people, but not to the extent of wiping them from the earth. Apparently Moses' pleading has some effect. Yet God also says something truly terrible. He tells Moses to take the people to the Promised Land without him. If he were to go with them, God says, he would likely destroy them on the way. The problem here is not with God but with Israel. Sinful people cannot live with a holy God.

As Moses intercedes again and asks God to go with them, he asks a rather remarkable thing of God. He asks God, "Please show me your glory" (Exod 33:18). And here we come to the reason we must read this part of the Bible over and over again if we are to understand the constancy of God's character.

'Glory' is a funny word. We don't use it very often, except perhaps of our sporting heroes. It's a word we probably most often associate with fame and dazzling lights. But what exactly does God's glory look like? How will God show his glory to Moses?

Listen to how he responds to Moses' request: "I will make all my goodness pass before you and will proclaim before you my name 'The LORD'" (Exod 33:19). So when Moses asks to see God's glory, God promises to proclaim his **name** to Moses. God's glory is tied up with his name. For most of us, names are about fashion—what was in vogue when our parents were naming us. But in the Scriptures, names are intimately connected with ideas and events and places and character. When God wants to display his character, he declares his name—because his name describes who he is.

The LORD descended in the cloud and stood with [Moses] there, and proclaimed the name of the LORD. The LORD passed before him and proclaimed, "The LORD, the LORD, a God merciful and gracious, slow to anger, and abounding in steadfast love and faithfulness, keeping steadfast love for thousands, forgiving iniquity and transgression and sin, but who will by no means clear the guilty, visiting the iniquity of the fathers on the children and the children's children, to the third and the fourth generation". And Moses quickly bowed his head toward the earth and worshiped. And he said, "If now I have found favour in your sight, O Lord, please let the Lord go in the midst of us, for it is a stiff-necked people, and pardon our iniquity and our sin, and take us for your inheritance". (Exod 34:5-9)

God's glory, all of God's goodness, is found in his name. God is the God who is loving and gracious and faithful. He is the God who keeps his promises and does what he says he will do. And for that reason Israel can give thanks, because he is the God who makes a way for sins to be forgiven.

But he will also punish wickedness and iniquity.

This second characteristic is just as important as the first. It is all very well to be forgiving. But we live in a broken world that thirsts for justice. Forgiveness with no justice is awful. In a world without righteousness and change, forgiveness becomes a license for persistent evil. But the God who loves and forgives will also finally and ultimately punish wickedness and evil.

SUFFERING WELL

Now we begin to see some of the reasons for rejoicing in God's sovereignty. When Habakkuk cries out and calls on God for justice, God is able to deliver it because he is powerful and because he is sovereign. God may not deliver his justice in the timing and manner we would choose; but he will surely deliver it. When we see injustice and horror and all the mess and muck of life in our world, we know, because of who God is, that one day there will be a reckoning. Judgement is not such a terrible thing in an evil world—especially judgement at the hands of a gracious and just God.

To sum up what we have seen: God's character is consistent. And this consistency means two things. It means the possibility of forgiveness, and the certainty of judgement leading to righteousness and justice.

How should we answer my friend Jacob's question? Is God really good? The first thing to say is that God's character is constant. God will not say today that white is white, but tomorrow that white is black. He is always implacably opposed to sin. And he will always act with grace and truth.

But this last statement requires us to go on to our second point about God's character. It is still possible that God's justice is evil. Maybe God **always** says that white is black!

The second guarantee of God's goodness lies in the way that his unchanging character has expressed itself towards his creation. To understand it properly, we need to remember again that God is in control of everything. He foreknows everything. He knows the past and the future in a way that we never can. For he does not simply **know** what will happen—he **determines** what will happen. For God to know the future is for God to purpose the future.

Stop and think about that with me for a moment.

"...I am God, and there is no other;
    I am God, and there is none like me,
declaring the end from the beginning
    and from ancient times things not yet done,
saying, 'My counsel shall stand,
    and I will accomplish all my purpose'". (Isa 46:9-10)

If this is true, then God knew from before the creation of the world that he would send his one and only Son to die for our sins. In fact, the Scriptures affirm this truth time and again.

"This Jesus, delivered up **according to the definite plan and foreknowledge of God**, you crucified and killed by the hands of lawless men." (Acts 2:23)

[Jesus] was **foreknown before the foundation of the world** but was made manifest in the last times for the sake of you who through him are believers in God... (1 Pet 1:20-21)

In the beginning was the Word, and the Word was with God, and the Word was God. (John 1:1)

From the very beginning, before that first precious word spoke the universe into being, God knew what was going to happen. God knew humanity would sin and fall. And

God knew he would send his one and only Son to die.

Jesus reminds us of this truth when he cries out to his Father in the hours before his crucifixion:

> "And now, Father, glorify me in your own presence with the glory that I had with you before the world existed." (John 17:5)

Jesus was not created. He was the Word that brought creation into being. Father and Son dwelt together in perfect union before the world was made. And they knew before the earth even existed that Jesus would come into this world as a man, to be glorified by his death and resurrection.

This is why it's no surprise to find that the Old Testament is full of promises about the coming of the Messiah, the true king, the son of David who would also be the Son of God. Isaiah did not fully comprehend what he was saying when he promised the coming of the one who would be called "Wonderful Counsellor, Mighty God, Everlasting Father, Prince of Peace" (Isa 9:6). Nevertheless, God spoke through him to declare to the world what would take place. The perfect Son, eternally begotten of the Father, was coming into the world. He was coming because that was what God had always planned.

But Isaiah also told us something else about Jesus: he was coming as the suffering servant. He was coming to die for the sins of his people. Jesus was coming to complete the mission that was his from before the foundations of the earth.

What do we learn when God finally becomes man;

when Jesus walks on this earth? We learn that light and darkness do not mix. In Christ we understand finally and fully that righteousness and injustice are implacably opposed to each other. Wherever Jesus speaks God's truth, God's enemies react in anger and hostility. The Pharisees and the Sadducees and all the rulers of Israel reject him. Yet at every step along the way, the light rules the darkness.

Jesus isn't surprised by the authorities' antagonism towards him. He isn't shocked when he is sentenced to crucifixion. He knows he must die. He teaches the disciples many times, "The Son of Man must suffer many things and be rejected by the elders and chief priests and scribes, and be killed, and on the third day be raised" (Luke 9:22). And so, "When the days drew near for him to be taken up, he set his face to go to Jerusalem" (Luke 9:51).

At every moment in the passion narrative, Jesus is in control. He knows he will be betrayed. He knows Peter will deny him. When the guards come to arrest him, they cower in fear before he gives them permission to take him prisoner (John 18:1-12). Even when he is brought before the Roman governor, Pilate, it is Jesus who is in control: "You would have no authority over me at all unless it had been given you from above" (John 19:11).

From before the foundation of the world, God knew his Son would come to die for us. Jesus lived his life as the one who had come to die. And his Father chose the time and place for him to fulfil God's purposes for his creation. The cross was not a mistake or a plan B or an afterthought. Not at any point.

Here we come face to face with one of the great mysteries of the universe—perhaps the greatest mystery of all. God created the world not only knowing people would sin and be condemned; not only knowing suffering and death would reign; but also knowing **he himself would be involved in the suffering**. He planned it and he planned that his Son would be a part of it.

This does not solve all of our problems. It will not remove suffering this side of Jesus' return. And it won't stop life hurting us, perhaps daily. But it does help us to pause before we accuse God of being a tyrant. The God who is the same yesterday, today and forever, planned to involve himself in the suffering of his creation, in order to glorify his Son and to display his glory and grace to every creature in heaven and on earth.

And as much as we may want to ask, "Why not do it without all the suffering?" the stark reality is that God has done it **this** way. Presumably this was the best way. Whatever else we might say, we must say this: God is not an evil young boy pulling the wings off flies. He did not make the world so he could revel in sadistic pleasure. But in some profound way (and here there are many mysteries), suffering is at the very heart of God's plan to create a perfect world and to glorify himself through his Son.

Jacob's question is an important question. Is God evil? But the answer is more important. No. God is not evil. He is the God who is the same yesterday, today and forever. He is the eternal Father, Son and Spirit who planned before the creation of the world to make a place where suffering would be essential to glory. And he displayed his love for his creation by sending Christ Jesus our Lord, who agonized in Gethsemane over the thought of facing the suffering that should be ours as a result of God's wrath on sin.

"For God so loved the world, that he gave his only Son, that whoever believes in him should not perish but have eternal life" (John 3:16): those immortal words mean more than we will ever be able to voice. But most assuredly they mean we have a God who can be trusted, even with suffering. Out of love for us, God chose that his Son would suffer. God included suffering in his plan to share his glory with us. So while suffering may be painful and awful, it comes from the hand of a sovereign God who will use it for good, and who guarantees that good by the gift of his Son.

And so we come to our next question: what does God's sovereignty over suffering mean for us as we seek to suffer well?

Providence and the cross

Perhaps most importantly, these truths about God help us to look in the right direction when we suffer. Suffering has always involved a question for human beings: does God love me? It was Job's question as he wrestled with the complete devastation of everything he held dear. It was the question that drove some of the psalmists to despair. How can the wicked prosper and the righteous struggle? It is a question that goes to the very heart of living in this world.

But it's a question that is often poorly answered. The problem is that suffering comes to us in the guise of God's providence, and providence is a particularly difficult thing to read. If God brings rain on the just and the unjust alike, how can life's experiences possibly be the basis for assessing whether or not God loves us?

Take my life as an example. I have two brothers and a sister whom I love and get on with. I had a happy and healthy childhood, although my knee once needed stitching when I tore it open on a rock in the backyard. I did well at school and enjoyed sport. I broke my finger and tore muscles in my back playing cricket (which has led to back pain on and off since then). In senior high school I dislocated my kneecap and needed surgery. But overall, nothing too tragic happened in my childhood— nothing except for the death of three of my grandparents while I was in primary (elementary) school.

I enjoyed life in high school. I had lots of friends, and it was during those years that I became a Christian. But I had a Christian friend who got early onset arthritis and gave up the faith. I also watched another friend's Christian parents split up. Through university and beyond I struggled with anxiety and depression. In the months before my first child was born, I suffered from panic attacks severe enough to hospitalize me. I've watched my father-in-law pass away at the age of 54 due to a brain tumour, and I've seen my mother come to know Jesus.

Lots of other things have happened in my life so far—good, bad and indifferent. But I don't need to list them all to make my point. My life is not particularly different from the lives of most of the people I know. We all have our ups and downs. In the midst of these ups and downs—in the midst of our uncomfortable world—how should we think about God's love for us? The answer is that we cannot read providence like a book. We do not know God's care and love for us by whether or not we have had a good day, or week, or month or even year.

The experiences of life do not tell us what God thinks of us. There is only one place we will unfailingly see the loving faithfulness of our Father in heaven. We must go to the cross, and we must see our Lord give up his life in love and rise in victory over death. That is the only place that will consistently show me how God thinks of me.

As Paul puts it in Romans 8:31, "If God is for us, who can be against us?" Why do we know that God is for us? We know because he "did not spare his own Son but gave him up for us all" (v. 32). Not even death can separate us from the love of God that is in Christ Jesus. So we must learn to look to the cross if we are ever to understand God's love.

This is precisely what the dear older saints at my church have taught themselves to do. When I talk to them about suffering, I see that they have learned not to be frightened of it or surprised by it. They know the God who is in control of all things. They do not claim to understand everything, but they are certain of God's love displayed in Christ. And they speak of clinging to the God who holds all things in his hands and who has, in Christ, revealed a day to come of overwhelming glory—even if it is a day that will come through great groaning.

The story so far

Having laid some crucial biblical foundations, we are now ready to move on and examine the surprising promises about suffering that God makes to his people. But before we do, let's remember what we have seen.

We live in a world full of increasingly faithless stories about God and suffering. These stories are training us to question God's word at every point. At best, they leave us with an insipid and ineffective God who stands on the sidelines and hopes like crazy that his children will find him. At worst, they lead us to believe there is no God at all. These stories lie to us and twist our view of truth. We have become so anxious to defend God against accusations of injustice that we have stopped reading parts of his word. We have stopped listening to what God says about himself.

If we are to truly understand suffering, we need to stop and listen again to the Scriptures. The God who made the world is the righteous, merciful and just God who stands in control of all things. This God has made a world that suffers. We suffer because of God's response to our sinfulness. Yet, in a miraculous and wonderful way, this same God has involved himself in our suffering. Through his Son, God promises us a share in his eternal glory. It is only with these truths firmly in place that we will be able to understand what God tells us about suffering as those who belong to Jesus.

Chapter 5

THE SURPRISINGLY PREDICTABLE SURPRISE

In the last few days, my son and I have started a new game. Unlike most games, this one doesn't require the consent of all parties. It's his game and I end up playing whether I like it or not. The aim of the game is to scare the living daylights out of Dad. He's getting quite good at it. Yesterday morning while I was making the bed, a hand shot out from under the bed frame and grabbed my ankle. I nearly hit the roof. A mischievous face appeared and burst into laughter. Apparently scaring your dad is a joy worth pursuing!

My son has reminded me that surprise is the essence of a good shock. The evening before the great monster-under-the-bed success, he tried unsuccessfully to hide in the laundry. I heard him rustling amongst the clothes on the floor before I got there and so wasn't surprised at all to find him lurking behind the door waiting to frighten me. When you know what to expect, the sting is taken out of fear.

But sometimes, even though we should have the right expectations, we get lazy. Having kissed my wife and kids goodbye this morning, I walked out from the kitchen to the front door. It was unlocked. We live in a reasonably safe part of town, but about a year ago we were broken into and so we're fairly security conscious. We don't make a habit of leaving the front door unlocked. I remember thinking that it was vaguely unusual to find it unlocked but I dismissed it almost immediately—one of the kids must have been a bit careless. Then, as I opened the door to head off to work, my son burst in from the front porch with a tremendous shout.

I shouldn't have been surprised. The game had been going on for days. I shouldn't have been surprised, because I knew he was going to try and scare me. But I was still caught completely off guard by his cunning plan. I should have expected it but I didn't. And because I didn't, I was caught off guard.

It seems to me that many of us are like this when it comes to suffering. If we have read our Bibles, we will know that suffering is not surprising. It is part of life in this world. Yet, for some reason, we still find it shocking. If we are going to suffer well, we need to explore again the biblical promises about suffering.

The promise of suffering

We have already seen one reason suffering shouldn't surprise us. We live in a world corrupted by sin. This creation stands rightly under the hand of God's judgement. We should expect death and all that goes with it, because we belong to Adam. This is a world where hurricanes destroy, floods drown and famines leech away life. God has told us that we live in a creation groaning under the weight of sin and longing for renewal. This side of Jesus' return, we should all expect suffering because our world is broken.

But in many ways, this makes the New Testament teaching on suffering even more surprising. While the Bible leaves us with no delusions about the broken nature of our world, in the pages of the New Testament this fallen nature of life is not particularly prominent. It's there; it just isn't mentioned or talked about very often.

What *is* talked about, and with alarming frequency, is a different form of suffering. Here it is from the lips of Jesus:

> "A disciple is not above his teacher, nor a servant above his master. It is enough for the disciple to be like his teacher, and the servant like his master. If they have called the master of the house Beelzebul, how much more will they malign those of his household." (Matt 10:24-25)

The great New Testament promise about suffering is not so much that all will suffer the pains and tribulations of a fallen world, but that suffering is guaranteed for those who follow a suffering Lord. This promise is made in so many ways and in so many places that it is impossible to avoid. In Jesus' last words to his disciples in John's Gospel, he spends much of his time preparing them not to be surprised by suffering.

> "If the world hates you, know that it has hated me before it hated you. If you were of the world, the world would love you as its own; but because you are not of the world, but I chose you out of the world, therefore the world hates you. Remember the word that I said to you: 'A servant is not greater than his master.' If they persecuted me, they will also persecute you. If they kept my word, they will also keep yours... I have said all these things to you to keep you from falling away. They will put you out of the synagogues. Indeed, the hour is coming when whoever kills you will think he is offering service to God. And they will do these things because they have not known the Father, nor me. But I have said these things to you, that when their hour comes you may remember that I told them to you." (John 15:18-20, 16:1-4)

And from Jesus on, suffering becomes foundational to apostolic teaching. Paul tells the Christians in Lystra, Iconium and Antioch, "through many tribulations we must enter the kingdom of God" (Acts 14:22). He writes to the Philippians, "it has been granted to you that for the sake of Christ you should not only believe in him but also suffer for his sake" (Phil 1:29). Paul reminds the Thessalonians that he has already told them about suffering. He specifically sent Timothy to encourage them:

...that no-one be moved by these afflictions. For
you yourselves know that we are destined for this.
For when we were with you, we kept telling you
beforehand that we were to suffer affliction, just as it
has come to pass, and just as you know. (1 Thess 3:3-4)

The apostle Peter exhorts the scattered saints of the dispersion:

...do not be surprised at the fiery trial when it comes
upon you to test you, as though something strange
were happening to you. But rejoice insofar as you
share Christ's sufferings, that you may also rejoice and
be glad when his glory is revealed. (1 Pet 4:12-13)

John writes from prison on Patmos as a "brother and partner in the tribulation and the kingdom and the patient endurance that are in Jesus" (Rev 1:9).

Paul's words to Timothy summarize the New Testament perfectly: "Indeed, all who desire to live a godly life in Christ Jesus will be persecuted" (2 Tim 3:12).

These brief quotations only just scratch the surface of the New Testament teaching on this issue. Even a half-hearted reader of the gospels and epistles couldn't fail to notice the promise. All Christians, without exception, must suffer. We should be as surprised about Christians suffering as I should have been when my son leaped through the front door. Hearing that Christians have suffered should strike us in the same way as learning that Bob went to the shops to buy milk this morning. It's not front-page news. It's normality.

The reason it's normal is not difficult to understand.

What would you expect to happen when the God who has been rejected and reviled for thousands of years steps into history as a man? John describes it as the coming of light and life into darkness. Thankfully, "The light shines in the darkness, and the darkness has not overcome it" (John 1:5). But these words reveal the friction. The darkness cannot overcome the light, but it continues desperately to try.

As we read the gospels, we see exactly what happens when the light steps into the darkness of this world. Jesus speaks truth, and the religious authorities send spies to trap him in his words. Jesus eats with tax collectors and cares for prostitutes, and the 'powers that be' accuse him of being a glutton and a drunkard. Jesus heals, and the Pharisees wish to kill. One of the great ironies of the gospels is that Jesus is hated because he does the right thing. It is ironic, but it is not surprising. And Jesus teaches us to expect the very same thing.

In the Sermon on the Mount, Jesus teaches his people what it means to be a disciple. For whom is the greatest blessing reserved? It is for those who are persecuted for righteousness' sake:

> "Blessed are you when others revile and persecute you and utter all kinds of evil against you falsely on my account. Rejoice and be glad, for your reward is great in heaven, for so they persecuted the prophets who were before you." (Matt 5:11-12)

When the grace and forgiveness won by Jesus enters into the lives of God's people, the Spirit transforms them to live for the sake of righteousness. If they killed Jesus because of his righteousness, what should we expect people to do to those who follow him?

The world hated Jesus' disciples back in the first century, and it is still the case at the beginning of the third millennium. I know of a man who was refused a promotion because he was too honest. He would not be involved in offering or receiving bribes when negotiating for business. I know another man who eats alone in the lunchroom more often than not because he is too good— the other blokes feel uncomfortable telling their crude jokes in front of him. Coming **to** Jesus means becoming **like** Jesus. If we are truly changed by the Spirit, our lives will be a stench to those around us.

That's not always true. In God's kindness, sometimes the beauty of godly living results in others finding salvation and life. But Peter knew what he was saying when he told the believers to "Keep your conduct among the Gentiles honourable, so that when they speak against you as evildoers, they may see your good deeds and glorify God on the day of visitation" (1 Pet 2:12). Peter knew that living as a Christian would mean being called evil. Suffering really shouldn't surprise us—at least, not if we know the one to whom we belong.

At this point, the keen-eyed observer may have noticed a small fly in the ointment. Quietly but surely, we have moved from speaking about suffering to speaking about persecution. Most of the book up until this point has been about suffering in general. We've touched on cancer, war and natural disasters, just to name a few of the many ways in which people suffer every day. Yet the biblical promise to Christians doesn't seem to be about getting sick or losing your life in a tsunami. Illness, disease and natural disasters were not at the forefront of Jesus' teaching about affliction. Nor did they loom large in the minds of the apostles.

This raises at least two significant issues. First, does the New Testament really say so little about general suffering in a fallen world? We need to look at the evidence for this idea. Second, if this really is the case, then what does it mean for how we suffer well as Christians?

Examining the biblical evidence

A negative statement is always harder to prove than a positive statement. It is easy to claim that elephants are grey: you find a book with elephant pictures in it and show me they're grey. It's much harder to claim there is no such thing as a pink elephant. How do you know? Have you seen every elephant that has ever lived? Could it be that there is a herd of pink elephants living in a remote jungle somewhere in South-East Asia, yet to be seen by human eyes?

As soon as I say that the New Testament is not particularly interested in the general suffering of a fallen world, our minds to jump to those passages where the New Testament clearly talks about such things. Towards the end of his ministry, Jesus tells his disciples that the last days will be full of earthquakes and famines and wars (Mark 13:7-8). When Paul details his own suffering, he talks about being cold and hungry and tired (2 Cor 11:21-29). In Romans 8, he spends lots of time talking about the groaning of this present creation. And James talks to believers about rejoicing when they face trials of **various** kinds (Jas 1:2-4). So why would I say that the New Testament is not particularly interested in the general suffering of creation?

Let me try and make my case.

The missing New Testament book

Perhaps more significantly than it might first seem, the New Testament contains nothing like the books of Job or Ecclesiastes. Job wrestles with what it means to suffer as an innocent man. The writer of Ecclesiastes contemplates the futility of life in the face of death. Both these books are concerned with the kind of suffering that we might classify as general suffering in a fallen world—the suffering of illness and accidents and famine and failure.

Since the Old Testament contains these books that wrestle so deeply with the nature of suffering, why don't we find similar books in the New Testament? Some might argue because the Old Testament has done such a good job of dealing with these things, there is no need for a New Testament equivalent. But this doesn't really account for the huge difference between the Old and New Testaments. Let's look at Ecclesiastes for a moment and compare it to what the New Testament teaches.

The big problem for the writer of Ecclesiastes is death. Death robs everything of its significance or, more specifically, its gain or profit. The question introduced in 1:3, "What does man **gain** by all the toil at which he toils under the sun?" becomes a refrain through the book (2:11, 2:22, 3:9, 4:4, 4:8, 5:16). And the answer is that there is no gain. No matter what human beings do—seek wisdom, chase pleasure, pursue fame, or work for wealth—it ultimately results in no lasting gain. Death means that whatever we achieve in this life is lost to us forever. Any gain is, at best, short term.

But to truly understand the author's point, we need to ask why this is the case. According to Ecclesiastes, there are two problems that cause this lack of gain. Firstly, there is the frustration of sometimes doing good things (e.g. planting crops) only to reap no reward (e.g. the crops are destroyed by a storm). Since we can't control the outcome of our actions, there is no guarantee of gain, even from hard work.

This means that sometimes our plans don't work out. A man will dig a pit, only to fall into it himself. The lumberjack will go out to split logs, only to be split by them (Eccl 10:8-9). And what was true before the coming of Christ is still true in these last days. As I write, the state of Queensland has recently been struck by a string of natural disasters. It started with widespread flooding, and then the biggest tropical cyclone to hit Australia in at least a century crossed the coast and headed inland. Photos of the devastation appeared in all the newspapers: cars and trucks swept away in the water; rooves ripped from homes as if someone had opened a tin can. Amidst it all, no photograph could capture the livelihoods lost.

In the aftermath of the cyclone, one reporter recorded footage of the local banana plantations. They were entirely destroyed by gale-force winds. This year there will be no crop and no income for the farmers. They have worked hard. They have acted with an eye on the future, but they will not harvest what they have sown. At this point, life in our world is just like life in the Old Testament world, and the truths of Ecclesiastes are unchanged.

However, this is the lesser of two great problems for the author of Ecclesiastes. The second and greater problem is that even if we act wisely and, in God's kindness, good things result, they are short lived. People and animals die, and nobody can know if there is any difference between them.

> I said in my heart with regard to the children of man that God is testing them that they may see that they themselves are but beasts. For what happens to the children of man and what happens to the beasts is the same; as one dies, so dies the other. They all have the same breath, and man has no advantage over the beasts, for all is vanity. All go to one place. All are from the dust, and to dust all return. Who knows whether the spirit of man goes upward and the spirit of the beast goes down into the earth? (Eccl 3:18-21)

According to Ecclesiastes, we don't know where we go when we die. The one thing we do know is that we can't take any of our fame, pleasure or wealth with us.

But here is where the gospel provides us with an entirely different perspective. Because of the coming of

Jesus, we know what will happen after death. Jesus is our forerunner. He faced death and God raised him to life. We know in Christ that death is not the end; it is the gateway to judgement for all, and to eternal life for those who trust in Jesus. The New Testament believer knows what the writer of Ecclesiastes did not know. Whatever might happen in this life, and no matter how insecure our temporal future may be, nothing can take our eternal home from us.

This changes things in a profound way. In Ecclesiastes the lack of gain means that life is vanity. Our actions are rendered almost meaningless because we will never really enjoy the fruits of anything we do. But for the apostle Paul, the resurrection means that living for Christ is never meaningless. Since we know that Christ died and rose again as the firstfruits, we are to be "steadfast, immovable, always abounding in the work of the Lord, knowing that in the Lord, your labour is not in vain" (1 Cor 15:58). Paul encourages believers who live in a world marked by death not to fret, but to continue to live in light of the hope that is ours in Christ.

It is easy for us to misunderstand the significance of this. Sometimes we forget that belonging to Christ does not guarantee comfort and happiness tomorrow. Some Christians want to promise us a victorious, pain-free life. But the New Testament promise is **not** that everything will be easy in this life. Sometimes life will be extremely painful. Christians are not exempt from God's hand of judgement at work in this fallen world. Just like our unbelieving neighbours, we will plant our crops and make our plans but they won't always come to fruition.

But—and this is a big, big but—in Christ we see life beyond death; we see life in the next world. Because Christ has been raised, our actions in the service of our Lord will result in glory on the day he visits us. When things are uncomfortable in this world, Christians are called on to live as those who have hope because Christ reveals God's future to us. We live for a world in which the uncertainty and terror of sin will be wiped away.

This explains why there is no Ecclesiastes in the New Testament. The Christian is not called on to wonder whether there is value in living for Christ in this world. The Christian does not need to ask whether our spirits will go up or go down. We know. And therefore we do not need to face death in the same way. Because of God's goodness in the gospel, we can say with Paul:

> ...we do not lose heart. Though our outer self is
> wasting away, our inner self is being renewed
> day by day. For this light momentary affliction is
> preparing for us an eternal weight of glory beyond all
> comparison, as we look not to the things that are seen
> but to the things that are unseen. For the things that
> are seen are transient, but the things that are unseen
> are eternal. (2 Cor 4:16-18)

The New Testament does not spend entire books wrestling with pain, suffering and death because, while entirely to be expected, they are transformed in light of the gospel. God has given us truth in Christ that genuinely changes our experience of life in a broken and fallen world. We are able, by the powerful working of God's gracious Spirit, to face death in a new way because of what God has revealed in Jesus. We do not need to fear death in the way our unbelieving neighbours do.

So here we have the first piece of evidence for my argument that the New Testament is more concerned with suffering for Jesus than with suffering in general: the New Testament does not contain anything like the big Old Testament books that deal with general suffering. And as we have seen, there is a good reason for this. But before we move on, it is important to deal with a significant misreading of the Bible that challenges this point.

What about the promise of healing?

Some Christians suggest that the New Testament doesn't spend much time talking about general suffering because in Christ we are freed from it. In Jesus, the new age has come. If we have enough faith then Christ will release us from that kind of suffering. The New Testament doesn't talk in the way that Job does, simply because the Christian should no longer get sick or face disaster. If Christ has come to bring in the new creation, then surely those who trust in the powerful king of the world will be free from the ravages of sin.

This argument has significant biblical support. If you were to search for words like 'sickness', 'disease' and 'illness' in the New Testament, you would come across lots and lots of references to people being healed. The gospels are full of stories about the blind and deaf and lame and dumb being totally cured by the power of

Jesus. What's more, the healing doesn't end there. The apostles did what Jesus did. Peter healed the lame man; Paul raised Eutychus from the dead. Surely we must conclude that the king of the world has given power to his people over the fallen-ness of this creation.

If all we had in our possession were the gospels and Acts, we could well be forgiven for thinking that Christ frees us from illness and suffering, and so we don't need to know about them. However, there is a significant problem. If you go searching for words like 'illness', 'sickness' and 'disease' (or 'healing', for that matter) in the **rest** of the New Testament, you will find very few references indeed. What's more, those references paint a very different picture.

For example, in 1 Corinthians 12 Paul mentions the gift of healing, but only in passing; he says almost nothing about it. And in James 5, James seems to suggest healing is possible—but the way to find it is by confessing your sins. Now, the New Testament does teach that in some cases sin and sickness are tied directly to each other (cf. 1 Cor 11:29-30). But these two references are surprising if guaranteed healing is to be a mark of New Testament Christian experience. Why don't the apostles tell us to be healed and show us how to do it?

The surprise is amplified by the other references to sickness and illness in the New Testament. We discover in 2 Timothy 4 that Paul left his missionary companion, Trophimus, behind in Miletus because he was ill (v. 20). It is a little strange that a faithful missionary should be left behind because he was not faithful enough to be healed. In 1 Timothy 5, Paul gives some advice to his trusted protégé Timothy about Timothy's apparently frequent gastro-intestinal ailments. Paul's advice is not to pray, but to drink a little wine. And in 2 Corinthians 12, we learn that Paul himself was inflicted with some sort of ailment that God chose not to take away. The apostle prayed in faith but was not healed. How should we explain this apparent indifference to sickness and healing?

We must see that the healing miracles in the gospels and Acts are a taste of the heavenly reality. While the coming of Christ as the king brings a glimpse of the kingdom, the rest of the New Testament does not teach that Christians should or will be free from the ailments of this life. Even Jesus himself assumes that Christians will get sick. When Jesus teaches his disciples about living at the end of the ages, he tells them that whatever they do to the least of Jesus' brothers, they do to Jesus. This includes visiting the sick (Matt 25:36). Jesus' passing comment clearly assumes that in the last days, there will still be brothers and sisters who need visiting because they are sick.

Of course, we have known all along that sickness is just a symptom of a world marked by death. We learn in the gospel that death and all that goes with it is passing away. But it won't be done away with until the end. Until then, our world is still a place where one hundred per cent of people still die. These physical bodies still waste away. God is powerful, and he may still intervene in our world to save people temporarily from illness. We would be faithless indeed to suggest otherwise. But even those people will die. God's promise in the gospel is that he will deal with all of this **when Jesus returns**.

For all of the wonderful pictures of the coming kingdom brought about through Jesus' healing ministry, the New Testament repeatedly teaches that we belong to a groaning world. In Jesus and the ministry of the apostles, we get a brief glimpse of the wonders of heavenly reality—a world where death and disease will melt away like snow in the face of spring. But in the meantime, our mortal bodies are still subject to the decays of this age. We shouldn't expect the full restoration of resurrection existence until we see Christ face to face on the last day. What a wonderful day that will be!

What happened to my favourite passage?

But let's get back to the main question of this chapter: is the New Testament more interested in the suffering that comes from belonging to Jesus than in the general suffering of life in a fallen world? So far, we've seen that the New Testament doesn't contain books like Job and Ecclesiastes—books that deal particularly with general suffering—because in Christ, God has revealed to us a more perfect future while also reminding us that this life will not be free of pain.

The next step is to look a little more closely at the kinds of suffering the New Testament **does** speak about. It is worth returning to the opening pages of this chapter and going slowly through the verses I mentioned there. You will see that Paul, Peter and John all talk at length about suffering for the sake of the kingdom. This teaching is woven into page after page of the New Testament, but we often mishear what is being said because we tend to read our own problems into the Bible. So let me encourage you to go back at some point and read those passages slowly and carefully.

But let's look now at one of the most popular and most significant passages about suffering in the New Testament: Romans 8. Many of us know at least one of the wonderful promises in this passage: that God works in everything for the good of those who love him. We may well have clung to that promise in the midst of great sadness. And without doubt, we ought to rejoice over the promise that "neither death nor life... will be able to separate us from the love of God in Christ Jesus our Lord" (Rom 8:38-39).

But even as we rejoice in these glorious promises, it is easy to read our situation into Romans 8 without reading what is actually there. Why does Paul talk here about the certainty of God's love, even in the face of death? **It is because belonging to Christ is a death sentence.** Becoming a Christian means taking up our cross and following Christ.

Just before these exalted promises in Romans 8 is a little section we often skip over in our preaching:

> The Spirit himself bears witness with our spirit that we are children of God, and if children, then heirs— heirs of God and fellow heirs with Christ, provided we suffer with him in order that we may also be glorified with him.
>
> For I consider that the sufferings of this present

time are not worth comparing with the glory that is to be revealed to us. (Rom 8:16-18)

We are used to the idea that by the Spirit we are children of God. And we are at least aware of the idea that the coming glory is not worth comparing to our present sufferings. But tucked away in these verses is the sting in the tail: **we will only be glorified with Christ if we also suffer with him.** And the suffering Paul has in mind here is not just the general suffering of getting sick or being caught in a tidal wave.

How do we know this? We see it in what Paul says at the end of Romans 8, where he talks about what threatens us. In verses 31 and following, Paul's expectation is that there will be enemies who stand against us, making accusations. His encouragement is that if you belong to God then God will protect you. Those who stand against you will ultimately fail. However, there will be a fight in this life— there will be tribulation, distress, persecution, famine, nakedness, danger and sword (v. 35).

This list is carefully crafted. It is not a series of words thrown together to cover the breadth of human suffering. It is a list that describes Paul's experience of living with Jesus as his Lord and preaching the truth about him. In fact, this list sounds just like the list in 2 Corinthians 11, where Paul talks about the hardship of being an apostle. For Paul, nakedness and famine were all part of walking the ancient world living for Jesus and speaking about him. This is confirmed for us in Romans 8 by the very next verse, which reads: "For your sake we are being killed all the day long; we are regarded as sheep to be slaughtered" (v. 36).

The apostle Paul personally experienced the reality of Jesus' promises. The servant will not be greater than the master (Matt 10:24-25). The godly Christian who wants to speak the truth about Christ will be attacked, ridiculed, maligned and mistreated. This is the promise for every believer. And because Paul really understood the cost of living and speaking for Christ, he wrote to encourage the believers to trust in the power of God's love.

It is not that Romans 8 has nothing to say to those who are suffering disease and illness. It is just that we fail to hear the main message when we forget to read it through the lens of the rest of the New Testament. Paul was writing to the Roman Christians to tell them to keep living for Jesus and honouring him—no matter what. He wrote because he knew that living for Christ is costly and painful. He wrote because he knew that the one great issue of life in the face of the coming of Christ is how we will respond to him.

Paul was not heartless. He cared for people and loved them greatly. Writing to the Philippians, Paul said that God protected him from great anguish by saving Epaphroditus from death. Paul was not ignorant of the suffering and sadness inherent in living in this world. He knew it from personal experience. But he also knew the great truth of the New Testament that our world wants to ignore: the only sure solution to our suffering can be found in Christ. For those who know the gospel, suffering and death are not a surprise. But more than that, the gospel brings life and hope to those who cling to Christ.

That is what the New Testament letters are all about. Paul wrote 1 Thessalonians to a church in which people got sick and died (4:13). His comfort for those still alive was the resurrection of Christ. But the great purpose of his letter was to encourage the Thessalonians to keep living for Jesus, no matter how much persecution they faced. Peter wrote 1 Peter to believers who were being maligned for following Jesus. They may have been suffering in many ways—bereavement, illness, business failure—but what they needed to hear was that living for Jesus and suffering for him is a badge of honour. Peter reminded them that suffering for the name of Christ was the indisputable sign that heaven was theirs. And so he exhorted them to cling to Christ and serve him, because Jesus is our only hope.

We will come back to think more about these issues in the last chapter. But for now, it is important for us to stop and see the big picture. When we come to the New Testament, much of the encouragement about suffering is not about general suffering in a fallen world; it's about the kinds of suffering we experience because we follow Christ. The apostles knew the temptations that might pull us away from Christ. They also knew that Jesus is our only hope. So they spent much of their time instructing believers about what truly living for Christ would be like.

Living for Jesus means suffering, because we live in a world of darkness that hates the light. We need to hear that whatever our circumstances, the most important thing is to continue trusting in Christ. More than that, we need to be reminded that belonging to Christ will lead to suffering. It's not a surprise; it's the only way to receive the inheritance.

To summarize: the coming of Jesus teaches us so much about suffering. It teaches us that suffering has an end; there will be a day when even death will be done away with. But it also teaches us that we get to that day by belonging to Jesus. And those who belong to him must expect not only the blessings of the new creation in the age to come, but also persecution in this present time. It is only when we are armed with this knowledge that we will be truly ready to suffer well.

Chapter 6

WHERE'S ALL THE PERSECUTION GONE?

"ALL WHO DESIRE TO LIVE A godly life in Christ Jesus will be persecuted" (2 Tim 3:12). It's a verse my old pastor drummed into me, and I'm profoundly thankful for it. But at the same time, it's a slightly surreal verse. The problem lies with that little word 'persecution'. What springs to your mind when you think of persecution?

For me, it's the stories of the great believers who gave their lives to the flames, or at the very least were exiled and imprisoned for their faith. The word 'persecution' throws up mental pictures of the likes of Latimer and Ridley, the great English reformers who were burned at the stake for refusing to let go of the truth of the gospel; or Polycarp, the second-century Bishop of Smyrna, who faced death rather than renouncing his trust in Christ.

The problem is that those wonderful stories of faith and conviction seem so far removed from my everyday experience. And I am sure I am not alone.

In my preparation for writing this book, I conducted a worldwide survey of people's experiences of suffering. The data was collected through an online survey site as a result of invitations sent to Matthias Media's customer database. About 880 people responded from around the globe. Although the majority of responses came from Australia and the USA, a reasonable number came from the UK and Europe and a smattering from Asia and Africa. Of those who responded, about 35% were pastors, while the rest were mainly active members of church. Roughly 37% were over 50, 54% were aged between 30 and 50, and the rest were under 30. Incredibly, the variation in results between these groups was very minor.

One of the key questions I asked was this:

In the Bible there seem to be two kinds of suffering:

1. suffering that happens to all people because they live in a fallen world (e.g. war, natural disaster, sickness, abuse, etc.)
2. suffering that happens specifically because people call themselves Christian (e.g. slander, ridicule, physical punishment, imprisonment, etc.).

On the scale below indicate the balance between these kinds of suffering in your own life.

People could choose one of the following five responses:

1. I suffer almost solely because I belong to Jesus.
2. I suffer somewhat more because I belong to Jesus than because I live in a fallen world.
3. There is about an even balance between suffering because I belong to Jesus and suffering because I live in a fallen world.
4. I suffer somewhat more because I live in a fallen world than because I belong to Jesus.
5. I suffer almost solely because I live in a fallen world.

Of all the respondents, only 11% chose the Jesus side of the equation (i.e. responses 1 and 2), and only 19% thought there was an even balance. That is, 70% of respondents thought they suffered somewhat more or almost solely because they live in a fallen creation than because they live as Christians.

These results aren't particularly surprising, but they do remind us of the distance that seems to exist between us and our New Testament counterparts. Would Paul and Peter have written the same kinds of letters if they'd been alive today? If John had been writing to 21st-century believers, would he have written more about the anguish of suffering through natural disasters than the threat of persecution and the challenge to stand firm in Christ?

As I've been arguing all the way through this book, I think we're in danger of being conned at this point. God revealed his truth through the apostles for his people in **all** ages. Part of our problem lies in our understanding of what the Bible means when it speaks about persecution—or more particularly, what the Bible has to say about suffering for Jesus. The word 'persecution' implies some sort of physical suffering. But it is only one of many words used to describe the experience of suffering for Christ.

This is much more important than it might at first seem. If whenever we think of suffering for Jesus we think of being beaten, shot at, imprisoned or put to death, then most of us living in the Western world will naturally think of the biblical teaching about suffering for our faith as almost irrelevant. But when we begin to investigate the New Testament teaching on suffering as a Christian, the language is much broader than the language of persecution. Let's start with Jesus himself.

In many ways, the Sermon on the Mount is 'Discipleship 101'. In the face of the gathering crowds and popularity that have developed around Jesus' ministry, Jesus takes his disciples aside and begins to teach them about what it truly means to live as members of the kingdom. His teaching is totally counter-cultural. The blessed ones are not the rich or the powerful or the famous; they are those who mourn and hunger for righteousness. They are those who are persecuted for righteousness' sake. But notice Jesus' words at the end of the Beatitudes:

> "Blessed are you when others revile you and persecute
> you and utter all kinds of evil against you falsely on
> my account. Rejoice and be glad, for your reward is
> great in heaven, for so they persecuted the prophets
> who were before you." (Matt 5:11-12)

Jesus does not reserve his encouragement just for those who are physically abused. To be **reviled** is to be blessed.[9] To have people **utter** all kinds of evil against us on account of Jesus is to be blessed. Jesus knew from the beginning that his followers would struggle as much with what we might now call mental and emotional abuse as they would with physical abuse. The same idea comes up in Matthew 10:

> "A disciple is not above his teacher, nor a servant above his master. It is enough for the disciple to be like his teacher, and the servant like his master. If they have called the master of the house Beelzebul, how much more will they malign those of his household." (vv. 24-25)

Even in the greatest of all discipleship calls—Jesus' call to take up our cross—the emphasis is not on physical hardship but on the danger of being ashamed:

> And calling the crowd to him with his disciples, he said to them, "If anyone would come after me, let him deny himself and take up his cross and follow me. For whoever would save his life will lose it, but whoever loses his life for my sake and the gospel's will save it. For what does it profit a man to gain the whole world and forfeit his soul? For what can a man give in return for his soul? For whoever is ashamed of me and of my words in this adulterous and sinful generation, of him will the Son of Man also be ashamed when he comes in the glory of his Father with the holy angels." (Mark 8:34-38)

---

9   To be 'reviled' is to be spoken to (or of) abusively.

When we think of suffering for Christ, 'persecution' is the word we naturally use. But in the Bible, the language is much more diverse. It talks of being reviled and spoken against and maligned. We read 'persecution' and think of being ready to die for Christ. The metaphor is correct, but our appreciation of it is dulled. We too seldom reflect on the everyday struggle of living for Christ. The Bible's big question for us is: will you obey Jesus and speak for him, or will you be ashamed of his words?

The importance of all this for our Christian lives is often highlighted for me in pastoral conversations. I remember one conversation with a godly, young Christian man about his work. He worked in the technology industry and his company was using pirated software to do their work. He felt embarrassed and ashamed about raising the issue, so he just chose to keep quiet. He didn't want to stand out.

I remember another conversation with a man who was thinking through what it meant to become a Christian, and felt challenged to change his sexual relationship with his non-Christian girlfriend. But he didn't want to do anything too radical in case he gave her a bad impression of Christianity. He was also worried people might think he was crazy.

These kinds of conversations are a regular feature of pastoring people in Jesus, and I am painfully aware of the temptation in my own life to stay quiet; the temptation not to rock the boat, not to do things that might seem too zealous. For several generations, our society has insisted that religion is a private affair—something between you and God. We are to avoid doing anything religious in

SUFFERING WELL

public that might cause people discomfort. We have been taught to 'live and let live', and so we're wary of any action that might cause embarrassment.

But the problem is that these situations happen every day. I am driving at the speed limit on a single-lane highway, and someone roars up behind me and drives right on my tail. Should I speed up so as not to cause offence, or obey the speed limit? My boss comes to see me because cash flow is tight. He just needs me to bill some 'extra' hours—hours I haven't worked—to the clients this month so we can get through. Will I give way to expedience, or speak the truth in love? On a day when I've arranged to pray with two mates at lunchtime, my workmates have been making jokes during the morning about the stupidity of Christianity. Do I tell them that I'm going to lunch or that I'm going to pray with my friends?

The great danger for Christians living in the West is not physical death at the hands of persecutors, but the slow, spiritual death of a thousand tiny compromises crouched at our door, waiting to devour our hearts. And one of the saddest predicaments of our age is that at the moment we need it most, we have let go of a robust theology of belonging to Christ and suffering for him.

I can think of at least four reasons for our lack of a theology of suffering. Firstly, compared to Christians in other parts of the world, we don't see ourselves as people who suffer particularly for Christ. And we feel this relative lack of suffering very deeply. We come to passages that speak about suffering for Christ, and we say things like, "We don't suffer very much in the West but we ought to give our money and prayers to those in Africa and Asia who suffer so deeply for their faith". It is right for us to stand beside those who suffer greatly for Christ in other countries. But we do not serve each other when we say we don't suffer, because it reinforces the idea that suffering for Christ is always about physical persecution. As a result, we fail to teach each other to live without shame in the face of the more subtle pressures in our culture.

Secondly, because Western culture has become obsessed with general suffering, we find ourselves spending much of our time defending how God can allow cancer and natural disasters. We spend much less time teaching each other from the Bible that God calls on us to live such godly lives for Jesus that people will dislike or even hate us for it.

Thirdly, we live in a world where abuse and reviling have become so commonplace as to hardly rate a mention. This struck me while reading a news story just last week. An entertainment reporter, Serene Branson, was covering the Grammy awards when she started to speak gibberish live on national television. Doctors believe she experienced a type of migraine that can cause confused speech. The story, which appeared in an online newspaper, was followed by nearly 150 comments.[10] Some ridiculed her. Some ridiculed the diagnosis.

---

10 'Grammys gibberish report explained', *The Sydney Morning Herald*, 18 February 2011, available online (viewed 22 February 2011): www.smh.com.au/lifestyle/wellbeing/grammys-gibberish-report-explained-20110218-1aypf.html

People called each other morons and idiots. A few called for restraint. The overall tone of the comments was awful, and that's not unusual.

We now live in a culture where anyone is free to make any comment they like on anything. And because the comments can be anonymous, people feel free to speak to each other in a way that they never would in person. Categories like 'vitriol' and 'revilement' are almost meaningless in the online world, because everyone is profoundly rude to each other. When it comes to using words, anything goes.

The effect is to reduce our sensitivity to the harshness of words. There is almost no category for libel or slander any more. And so we Christians feel that we shouldn't worry about having a few choice words tossed our way—after all, sticks and stones can break your bones but names can never hurt you. To worry about being ridiculed or reviled these days makes you a wimp or oversensitive. But God doesn't look at it like that. The New Testament has a lot to say about standing up for Christ in the face of angry, abusive words. Perhaps we need to say more.

Finally, we use clever theological arguments to excuse our disobedience when it comes to suffering for Jesus. The "all things to all people" excuse is one of the best. Of course it is vital for us to hear Paul's wonderful encouragement in 1 Corinthians 9 to put no cultural barrier in the way of people hearing about Jesus. Paul could become a Jew to Jews and a Gentile to the Gentiles because many of the cultural differences were irrelevant to the gospel. The first-century Jewish Christians needed to learn to eat non-kosher food for the sake of welcoming their brothers and sisters in Christ, and there are many valid applications of this principle in our own context.

But this truth also provides us with a wonderful excuse to cover up ungodliness. "In order to get on with the blokes at work," we say, "I need to swear occasionally. In fact, one of the young guys told me he was thinking more positively about Christians because I was able to tell a few crude jokes." Somewhere along the way we have lost Paul's injunction to "let there be no filthiness nor foolish talk nor crude joking, which are out of place, but instead let there be thanksgiving" (Eph 5:4).

We could multiply the examples here, but I have probably said enough. Being all things to all men is never an excuse in the Bible to act in an ungodly way. Ungodliness never promotes the gospel; it just makes people *like* us more. We need to be able to distinguish between the praise of men and the praise of God.

For all of these reasons, and perhaps more, our theology of suffering for belonging to Jesus is largely lacking. How should we respond?

The right response shouldn't really surprise us. We must do what God always calls us to do: we must listen again to what he says.

Firstly, this will mean letting the New Testament voice about suffering be heard. So let me remind you again of a number of passages we have already seen.

Jesus taught his disciples:

> "A disciple is not above his teacher, nor a servant
> above his master. It is enough for the disciple to be
> like his teacher, and the servant like his master. If they
> have called the master of the house Beelzebul, how
> much more will they malign those of his household."
> (Matt 10:24-25)

If we belong to Jesus, then people will treat us like they treated Jesus. There can be no other expectation in a world marked by sinful rebellion. If we genuinely want to speak the truth in love and live like our Lord Jesus lived, then people will hate us for it. So we need to remember that the maligning, revilement, ridicule, persecution and even death that may come as a result are not terrors to be avoided, but signs from God to be received with joy. Let us listen again to Jesus:

> "Blessed are you when others revile you and persecute
> you and utter all kinds of evil against you falsely on
> my account. Rejoice and be glad, for your reward is
> great in heaven, for so they persecuted the prophets
> who were before you." (Matt 5:11-12)

When we get hurt for doing the right thing, the comfort of the gospel is that the pain is a sign of who we truly are. Just as an athlete who never aches after training is not a real athlete, and a soldier who is never scarred by battle is not a real soldier, so a Christian unmarked by suffering is not a real child of God. That is why these words of Jesus are echoed in so many places by the apostles:

Only let your manner of life be worthy of the gospel of Christ, so that whether I come and see you or am absent, I may hear of you that you are standing firm in one spirit, with one mind striving side by side for the faith of the gospel, and not frightened in anything by your opponents. This is a clear sign to them of their destruction, but of your salvation, and that from God. For it has been granted to you that for the sake of Christ you should not only believe in him but also suffer for his sake, engaged in the same conflict that you saw I had and now hear that I still have. (Phil 1:27-30)

For we know, brothers loved by God, that he has chosen you, because our gospel came to you not only in word, but also in power and in the Holy Spirit and with full conviction. You know what kind of men we proved to be among you for your sake. And you became imitators of us and of the Lord, for you received the word in much affliction, with the joy of the Holy Spirit, so that you became an example to all the believers in Macedonia and in Achaia. (1 Thess 1:4-7)

Beloved, do not be surprised at the fiery trial when it comes upon you to test you, as though something strange were happening to you. But rejoice insofar as you share Christ's sufferings, that you may also rejoice and be glad when his glory is revealed. If you are insulted for the name of Christ, you are blessed, because the Spirit of glory and of God rests upon you. (1 Pet 4:12-14)

So we do not lose heart. Though our outer self is wasting away, our inner self is being renewed day by day. For this light momentary affliction is preparing for us an eternal weight of glory beyond all comparison, as we look not to the things that are seen but to the things that are unseen. For the things that are seen are transient, but the things that are unseen are eternal. (2 Cor 4:16-18)

It is impossible to read the Scriptures without realizing that living for Christ will mean suffering. But it's also impossible to miss the **promise** of suffering. Those who truly belong to Jesus will share not just in the pain of his ministry in this world, but also in the joy of his ministry in the next. We must teach this to each other from the very moment of conversion. We must share this truth with our children so they grow up rejoicing that they're counted as Christ's when they suffer for him.

Secondly, as we read and teach these passages to each other, we must avoid gently twisting passages to say what we want to hear. We must let the voice of passages like Romans 8 and 2 Corinthians 4 be heard. It is so much easier to hear and to teach each other that Romans 8 is about trusting Christ in our cancer rather than living obediently for Jesus even when people hate us for it. Likewise, Paul's encouragement in 2 Corinthians 4 that we have the gospel treasure in jars of clay is not primarily about our depressive tendencies; it is about the fact that Paul was afflicted, crushed, persecuted and struck down for speaking about Jesus and living for him. And Paul calls us to imitate him as he imitates Jesus (1 Cor 11:1). We must see and accept the primary applications of these passages rather than just reading our own circumstances into them.

Finally, a real biblical theology of suffering will only be ours as we resist the temptation to dismiss or ignore the pressures we experience as Western Christians. We must certainly call on each other to stand beside our persecuted brothers and sisters in parts of the Middle East, Asia and Africa, but we must also remind each other that we also face real, if more subtle, pressures to compromise our faith.

We must let the New Testament teaching about shame and revilement take its rightful place in our encouragement of each other, so that we will have the strength to resist temptation when it comes our way. The fact that our suffering is less physical than others' does not mean it is less important or less real. We must encourage each other not to give in to shame, and we must ask God's Spirit to enable us to live faithfully as servants of our crucified king.

Chapter 7

SUFFERING, SIN AND THE GLORY OF GOD

In the previous chapter, I mentioned a survey of Christian suffering I conducted. As part of that survey, I asked people to share a brief description of their worst experience of suffering. Reading through all the responses was overwhelming. The weight of what people shared was totally out of proportion with the brevity of their responses. One woman was molested by her grandfather and lost her sister when she was four years old. Another person contracted viral encephalitis as an 18-year-old and has since suffered short-term memory loss and epilepsy. Another man told us that his wife had committed suicide and his 21-year-old son had died in an accident.

Hundreds of people told us about their miscarriages, sickness, abuse and divorce—to name but some of the more common kinds of suffering people wrote to us about. The effect of reading these short descriptions of suffering, one after the other, was a strange combination of poignancy and absence. I was struck by the sheer volume of human suffering in our world. At the same time, the weight of all that suffering felt beyond my ability to comprehend. It was easier to turn my emotions off.

But you cannot ignore the burning question in the face of all of that pain: what should we do with it?

This was one of the greatest challenges I experienced in writing this book. Is it possible to write mainly about suffering for Jesus when so much other suffering is taking place? In the face of such a weight of suffering, is it fair to just emphasize suffering for Jesus? What connection, if any, is there between our general suffering and our suffering for Christ?

These are the questions to which we must now turn. But please remember that even here, we must be ready to listen to the answers God gives us rather than the ones we long to hear.

Our question in this chapter, then, is this: as much as we need to read the New Testament on its own terms and listen to its challenges to live for Christ, does the Bible say anything that might help us to live Christianly in the face of the general sufferings of a fallen world?

The key to answering this question lies in a slightly unexpected place: God's promises to discipline his children. To understand these properly, we will begin by looking at Hebrews 12 in some detail. You will probably follow more of what we are about to explore if you pause here and read Hebrews 12 for yourself before we start, and then refer to it again as we go.

Suffering as legitimate children

I have suggested that Hebrews 12 will help us learn how, as Christians, to cope with general suffering. But we need to begin by noting that, yet again, Hebrews 12 is primarily about suffering for belonging to Christ. Hebrews is a letter written to people in danger of letting go of Jesus. We know from 6:9-10 that the Hebrew Christians had a history of serving their brethren and clinging to Christ. As we read further, we find that this service involved standing by their suffering fellow Christians and sometimes suffering themselves:

> But recall the former days when, after you were enlightened, you endured a hard struggle with sufferings, sometimes being publicly exposed to reproach and affliction, and sometimes being partners with those so treated. (Heb 10:32-33)

Hebrews is written to people who have suffered greatly for belonging to Christ. But the reason for writing the letter is a sad one. These people who have persevered through so much are now in danger of letting go of their commitment to Christ. Hebrews is written to encourage them to persevere, to keep putting him first and to live for him, no matter what suffering might come.

Hebrews 12 is a crucial part of the argument of the letter. Its primary aim is to encourage these Christians to hold on to Christ. It opens with a call to look to Jesus and his example in suffering.

> Therefore, since we are surrounded by so great
> a cloud of witnesses, let us also lay aside every
> weight, and sin which clings so closely, and let
> us run with endurance the race that is set before
> us, looking to Jesus, the founder and perfecter of
> our faith, who for the joy that was set before him
> endured the cross, despising the shame, and is
> seated at the right hand of the throne of God.
>
> Consider him who endured from sinners such
> hostility against himself, so that you may not grow
> weary or fainthearted. (Heb 12:1-3)

The author is convinced that in God's grace, it is only considering Jesus and his response to suffering that will encourage us to persevere when we suffer. Here, as in many other passages we have seen, the emphasis is on suffering at the hands of those opposed to God. But notice how the writer describes the danger to their Christian life: they are growing weary and fainthearted.

As I read those words, I am reminded of the end of a long morning at the shops with young children. You say, "Just one more errand to run", and your three-year-old sits down in the middle of the footpath and refuses to go on. It's not just that his legs are tired and his feet are sore; his will is defeated. His feet are physically capable of taking another step, but his heart cannot see the purpose. Doing tiring, difficult things over and over again often brings us to the point of surrender.

The danger for the Hebrews is that they are nearing this point in their Christian faith. They have honoured Christ and been ridiculed. They have stood up for their

SUFFERING WELL

faith and been afflicted. They have visited their brothers and sisters in prison and so shown themselves to be deserving of the same fate. And this constant battering has resulted in that feeling of hopelessness most of us have experienced at one time or another. But this hopelessness is much worse than any other. It is leading them to question their commitment to Christ. Is it worth clinging to Jesus?

In order to encourage them, the writer of Hebrews returns to an idea that we have seen in many other places: God's promise that suffering leads to joy. Christ suffered great pain, but he persevered because of the offer of long-term gain. Jesus knew that God's ultimate end was joy—the joy of wholeness and righteousness, the joy of a new creation restored in worship of the living God. And because Jesus knew his goal, he was willing to persevere through the shame of going to the cross—the shame of standing under the curse of God.

This Jesus is our ultimate example. He is our reminder that perseverance brings its rewards according to the promises of God.

If I was trying to encourage the Hebrews, I suspect I would have finished at this point. But the writer of Hebrews is only just getting started. He has a lot more to say. Having told them to look to the example of Jesus, he then rebukes them for their sinfulness: "In your struggle against sin you have not yet resisted to the point of shedding your blood" (12:4). Surely Jesus' great example of perseverance for the sake of glory is all we need. But no—the writer of Hebrews wants us to think about something else. Have we yet struggled like Jesus struggled?

It is a confronting, in-your-face kind of question. And the more you ponder the passage, the more outrageous you realize it is. These people are tottering on the edge of giving up their faith because they are suffering for living for Christ. People are ridiculing them, persecuting them and threatening them with prison. Their external circumstances seem almost unbearable. But where does the author of Hebrews tell us the real issue is? Is it with the evil authorities who have thrown them into prison and confiscated their property? It is not. The real problem lies in their sinful hearts. Have they struggled enough against sin? Have they struggled against sin to the point of shedding blood?

My first reaction to this rebuke is indignation. How pastorally insensitive! Why give these struggling Christians such a slap in the face? Yet here is the wisdom of God. As these people suffer, what really matters? It is whether they will stick with Christ or let him go. And so the great struggle of suffering is not particularly with outside powers and forces, but with our stubborn, sinful hearts.

This is not a particularly fashionable response to the problem of suffering. Are you struggling to cling to Christ in the face of persecution? Repent! It's certainly not the kind of pastoral advice that leaps readily to mind when consoling the suffering. But it would seem, at least in this instance, to be part of God's wisdom. And the reason for this is revealed as the passage goes on.

According to the rest of Hebrews 12, suffering is a gift from God to his children. It is the mark of being God's children, because God uses suffering to raise children who will rejoice in the peaceful fruit of righteousness. What is required to form us and mould us into the people God wants us to be? It is the good gift of suffering.

Any parent knows the necessity of pain in raising children of honesty, wisdom and integrity. As uncomfortable as it is, I do not always step in to protect my children from difficult friends who are hard work to get on with. My children need to learn to deal with it for themselves. When my children fight with each other I do not always separate them, because they need to learn how to responsibly resolve the problem. When a teacher unjustly accuses them of doing wrong and puts them on detention, I do not rush into school to plead their cause. I encourage them to suffer the punishment quietly and patiently. Why? Because I have seen the results of people who have always been saved from difficulty—people who have never gained the resources to deal with the problems that crop up in life.

Graciousness, wisdom, integrity, godliness, faithfulness... none of these things is learned in comfort. We grow in them not when times are easy but when times are raw and hard. And so the passage teaches us that our Father in heaven will bring difficulty into our lives to transform us into people who look like Jesus:

> And have you forgotten the exhortation that addresses you as sons?

> "My son, do not regard lightly the discipline of the
>   Lord,
>   nor be weary when reproved by him.
>   For the Lord disciplines the one he loves,
>   and chastises every son whom he receives."
>
> It is for discipline that you have to endure. God is
> treating you as sons. For what son is there whom
> his father does not discipline? If you are left without
> discipline, in which all have participated, then you are
> illegitimate children and not sons. (Heb 12:5-8)

God brings suffering into our lives in order to discipline us, because he loves us and wishes to train us by it. And here we begin to see the link between suffering for Christ and the general suffering of living in this fallen creation. Whenever suffering comes along—of whatever kind—the right way to deal with it lies in staying true to Christ. Being ridiculed for believing in Christ or thrown in prison for refusing to deny his name bring particularly acute challenges to trusting him, but in all suffering we are presented with the one challenge: the challenge to faithfully follow Christ.

The connection with general suffering

This is why, while much of the New Testament focuses on the challenge of suffering particularly for Jesus, it also encourages us to live well in the face of general suffering. One particularly interesting example occurs in the book of James:

> Count it all joy, my brothers, when you meet trials of
> various kinds, for you know that the testing of your
> faith produces steadfastness. And let steadfastness
> have its full effect, that you may be perfect and
> complete, lacking in nothing. (Jas 1:2-4)

Do you notice that James does not specify precisely what kind
of suffering he is talking about? He just tells us to rejoice
when we meet trials "of various kinds". This is because
even in the general trials of life, our challenge is to be godly.
In James's context, one of the particular trials on view is the
trial of temptation. The people James is writing to are not
suffering from persecution; they are just struggling with
their own sinfulness. They are experiencing temptation,
and we can guess how they've responded from what
James says to them: "Let no-one say when he is tempted,
'I am being tempted by God'" (1:13). These Christians have
blamed God for putting temptation in their way. But James
makes it very clear that they are experiencing temptation
not because God is making life difficult, but because they
are sinful: "Each person is tempted when he is lured and
enticed by his own desire" (1:14).

These people have suffered because of their own
nature, and they have been arrogant enough to blame
God. But here is a great sign of the wonder and generosity
of our God. God tells them that even as they face the
temptation caused by their own sinfulness, he is willing
to use it for their good in Christ.

What is James's advice to those struggling with
temptation? When you struggle with the pain and difficulty

of your own disobedience, don't blame God but persevere in doing good. At the same time, give thanks for the trial because "the testing of your faith produces steadfastness" (1:3), and "blessed is the man who remains steadfast under trial, for when he has stood the test he will receive the crown of life, which God has promised to those who love him" (1:12).

In God's grace and kindness, he will use even the struggle and pain of wrestling with our sinful desires to lead us to maturity and godliness. How good is God, that he even uses our own sinfulness to make us like Christ? When we are tempted to grumble and whinge about life, we do well to remember God's kindness towards us. God's promise to work all things together for our good is fulfilled in ways we could never even begin to imagine.

But God's blessings in suffering extend beyond using the suffering brought about by our own sinfulness. God will use **all** suffering to bring about our good:

> Therefore, since we have been justified by faith, we have peace with God through our Lord Jesus Christ. Through him we have also obtained access by faith into this grace in which we stand, and we rejoice in hope of the glory of God. Not only that, but we rejoice in our sufferings, knowing that suffering produces endurance, and endurance produces character, and character produces hope, and hope does not put us to shame, because God's love has been poured into our hearts through the Holy Spirit who has been given to us. (Rom 5:1-5)

By the power of God's Holy Spirit, all suffering provides

us with an opportunity to honour Christ, because suffering is part of God's design. It is part of the way he has chosen to work in us for our good and for his glory.

What is God doing in us for our good and for his glory? He is shaping godly character. And what are the temptations we face as we suffer? We face the temptation to grumble against God, to doubt God's goodness, to use our current difficulty to excuse our ungodliness—whether it be overeating or porn or the escape of alcoholic oblivion. Suffering reveals our hearts and calls us to trust deeply in God's work as we battle with our sinfulness and self-centredness.

At the very moment when life is most uncomfortable, God encourages us. God's word tells us that these moments teach us to be like Christ. They train us to endure, they shape our character and they ignite our hope. Peter captures the idea in slightly cryptic words when he says:

> Since therefore Christ suffered in the flesh, arm yourselves with the same way of thinking, for whoever has suffered in the flesh has ceased from sin, so as to live for the rest of the time in the flesh no longer for human passions but for the will of God. (1 Pet 4:1-2)

There is a connection between suffering and ceasing from sin. Those who wish to avoid suffering will dance to the beat of the world (i.e. they will keep on sinning). But those who wish to honour God will suffer. Those who are suffering as Christians are those who are now obeying God's will rather than their own fleshly passions.

In nearly every moment of suffering, Christians face the question: will you stick with Jesus or will you walk in the way of comfort? Sometimes the question comes to us overtly, as people ridicule us or even physically abuse us for belonging to Christ. Sometimes the question is subtler: wouldn't it be easier to give in to sexual temptation right now than to resist? Sometimes the question comes in the mind-numbing awfulness of pain: as Job's wife said to him, "Do you still hold fast your integrity? Curse God and die" (Job 2:9).

But whatever the situation, the encouragement still stands. As God graciously enables us through his word and by his Spirit to live for Christ, he is slowly scouring away our sin and making us like Jesus.

Perhaps our greatest problem is our failure to realize the treasure God is producing by this refining. To be like Jesus is our goal as human beings—it is God's purpose for our lives. And as we become like him, we bring glory to the glorious creator and sustainer of the world. Peter puts it like this:

> Blessed be the God and Father of our Lord Jesus Christ! According to his great mercy, he has caused us to be born again to a living hope through the resurrection of Jesus Christ from the dead, to an inheritance that is imperishable, undefiled, and unfading, kept in heaven for you, who by God's power are being guarded through faith for a salvation ready to be revealed in the last time. In this you rejoice, though now for a little while, if necessary, you have been grieved by various trials, so that the tested

genuineness of your faith—more precious than gold that perishes though it is tested by fire—may be found to result in praise and glory and honour at the revelation of Jesus Christ. Though you have not seen him, you love him. Though you do not now see him, you believe in him and rejoice with joy that is inexpressible and filled with glory, obtaining the outcome of your faith, the salvation of your souls. (1 Pet 1:3-9)

In his infinite wisdom, God is testing and refining our faith through all of our sufferings, that we might be revealed to the whole world as his creation for his glory and honour. And even as God refines us and makes us like our Lord who suffers, he is preparing us for glory. He is making us ready to stand in his presence as the inheritors of the new creation.

What does God want to say to those who suffer under the pains and pangs of a cursed creation? What words does he speak to all of us as our outer selves waste away? Whether our sufferings at this moment are the general sufferings of living in the world, the sufferings brought about by the warring sinfulness of our own souls, or the particular sufferings of living for Jesus in this groaning creation, God says the same thing to each of us: 'Prayerfully trust in me. Honour Christ. Do what is good.'

Therefore let those who suffer according to God's will entrust their souls to a faithful Creator while doing good. (1 Pet 4:19)

This shouldn't surprise us. It's just what Jesus did:

> He committed no sin, neither was deceit found in
> his mouth. When he was reviled, he did not revile
> in return; when he suffered, he did not threaten, but
> continued entrusting himself to him who judges
> justly. He himself bore our sins in his body on the
> tree, that we might die to sin and live to righteousness.
> By his wounds you have been healed. For you were
> straying like sheep, but have now returned to the
> Shepherd and Overseer of your souls. (1 Pet 2:22-25)

Chapter 8

THE CHAPTER THAT DOESN'T QUITE BELONG

IN ONE OF MY PREVIOUS JOBS, I worked in a slightly eclectic part of Sydney. I was working for a Christian publishing house in an office on the first floor. Downstairs on one side was a speech pathologist and on the other side was a gaudy looking Italian restaurant that looked a bit like it was trying to celebrate Valentine's Day all 365 days of the year. Around the corner was a carpet warehouse. The carpet warehouse was particularly fascinating because every few months a sale sign would appear out the front. Not that there's anything amazing about a carpet warehouse having sales—it's just that they weren't selling carpet. One month they had boxes and boxes of discounted running shoes. I could see no obvious connection with carpets. I guess the store's owner came across a shipment of cheap trainers and hoped to make a buck. Or maybe they fell off the back of a truck.

Sometimes we come across things in life that seem totally out of place; there's really no logical reason for them. At other times we come across things that make sense, even if they're out of place—like the little rack of CDs beside the counter at my local service station. They don't quite belong beside the chocolate bars and various pieces of car-associated paraphernalia that adorn the counter, but you understand why they're there. Someone is buying petrol on a long trip and feeling bored. Maybe they will buy a CD to while away the hours.

This chapter is a bit like that CD rack. It's here because it considers things in the New Testament about suffering that are good for us to understand. The only problem is that these things don't quite fit into the logic of the rest of the book. So before we move onto the final chapters of the book, where we will explore in greater depth what it means to suffer well, here is the chapter that doesn't quite fit.

It's suffering for Christ, but it's not persecution

As we've seen, Christians will suffer in two ways. We will suffer along with the rest of the world because we live in a fallen creation. And we will suffer because we seek to live faithfully for Jesus in a world that rejects him. But there is a third category of suffering worth highlighting. This kind of suffering occurs because we are God's people, but it isn't related to persecution. It is the sorrow of seeing the world through God's eyes.

I can think of three forms of this kind of suffering. The first involves the awfulness of watching people wallow in their sins. The story of Lot is a great biblical example of this kind of sadness. In 2 Peter 2:7-8, Lot is described as being "greatly distressed by the sensual conduct of the wicked (for as that righteous man lived among them day after day, he was tormenting his righteous soul over their lawless deeds that he saw and heard)". This does not seem to be a description of Lot's persecution by the wicked. It is simply describing Lot's distress at the folly of sinfulness lived large.

The author of the awe-inspiring Psalm 119 provides another example. His love of God's law, and his meditation on the goodness and perfection of God's ways, lead him to grieve over those who reject God: "My eyes shed streams of tears, because people do not keep your law" (v. 136).

For the godly conscience, there is something very sad about seeing family and friends and even just casual acquaintances living sinfully. Hearing of a workmate's drunken escapades over the weekend doesn't provoke laughter or joy. It simply brings disappointment and sadness. Hearing of your non-Christian friend's string of disasters with boyfriends she has slept with in order to find love brings a sense of emptiness and distress, even as you try to offer wisdom and console her.

Because Christians love Jesus and have God's word, we know what the good life looks like. So when we see the sinful folly of our family and friends, it leads naturally to a sense of brokenness and despair. To put it simply, compassion is another source of suffering for those who live for Christ. Even when we are not being persecuted, we will still feel the heaviness that comes from watching sin destroy lives.

Which brings us to the second sadness detailed in the pages of the New Testament: the sadness of longing for the salvation of others but seeing no change. Our Lord Jesus knew this distress as he came to Jerusalem at the end of his ministry:

> And when [Jesus] drew near and saw the city, he wept over it, saying, "Would that you, even you, had known on this day the things that make for peace! But now they are hidden from your eyes. For the days will come upon you, when your enemies will set up a barricade around you and surround you and hem you in on every side and tear you down to the ground, you and your children within you. And they will not leave one stone upon another in you, because you did not know the time of your visitation." (Luke 19:41-44)

The apostle Paul experienced a similar anguish over his own countrymen:

> I am speaking the truth in Christ—I am not lying; my conscience bears me witness in the Holy Spirit—that I have great sorrow and unceasing anguish in my heart. For I could wish that I myself were accursed and

cut off from Christ for the sake of my brothers, my
kinsmen according to the flesh. (Rom 9:1-3)

People who are being genuinely changed by the Holy
Spirit will always feel a longing for their friends and
family to know Jesus. And because the stakes are so
high—eternal judgement or eternal salvation—these
things weigh deeply on our hearts. Our non-Christian
neighbours do not share these worries, but they are real
concerns for many Christians I know.

Part of the reason I raise this kind of sadness is to
acknowledge that it adds to the discomfort of living for
Christ. And over time it easily generates in some people
a weariness that leads them to question and doubt their
commitment to Christ. We need to remind each other
that these feelings are right feelings to have. In fact, they
are some of the most profoundly Christian feelings it is
possible to have, because they are the feelings of our Lord.

The solution to feeling like this is to continue to ask God
to have mercy on our world, and to seek the appropriate
opportunities to share the truth about Christ. We must
learn to be humble enough to know that salvation is
in God's hands, yet we must not cope by turning all of
our feelings off. It is right to have compassion on our
neighbours and to pray for their salvation. That is part of
the burden of living for and knowing Christ.

This longing for others' salvation relates very closely to
the third way in which we experience sadness for belonging
to Christ, which is the sadness of seeing Christian brothers
and sisters living sinfully and rebelliously. Again, we see

this pain deeply in the apostles' hearts. Paul speaks about the difficulties of living as an apostle of Christ:

> And, apart from other things, there is the daily
> pressure on me of my anxiety for all the churches.
> Who is weak, and I am not weak? Who is made to fall,
> and I am not indignant? (2 Cor 11:28-29)

In another letter, Paul describes his anguish at not knowing whether one of the churches he had established was still standing firm in Jesus:

> Therefore when we could bear it no longer, we were
> willing to be left behind at Athens alone, and we
> sent Timothy, our brother and God's co-worker in
> the gospel of Christ, to establish and exhort you in
> your faith, that no-one be moved by these afflictions.
> For you yourselves know that we are destined for
> this. For when we were with you, we kept telling you
> beforehand that we were to suffer affliction, just as
> it has come to pass, and just as you know. For this
> reason, when I could bear it no longer, I sent to learn
> about your faith, for fear that somehow the tempter
> had tempted you and our labour would be in vain.
> (1 Thess 3:1-5)

Because God's people share God's heart for the world, we will be concerned over many things that the world has no care about at all. As we become more like Jesus, some of the pain of living in this fallen world will, by God's grace, strike us even more deeply. We will long for the salvation of our friends; and we will mourn over Christians who are making wayward decisions.

We need to be encouraged to see that these feelings are right. We need to know that suffering well will involve understanding these issues rightly. We must ask God to graciously help us resist the temptation to give up Christ that comes even with godly sufferings.

I have seen some Christians so distressed by their family's rejection of Jesus that they start to doubt his goodness. They say, "If God will not save my family, I do not want to be part of his family". At this point, it is vital for us to grasp Paul's response to the anguish he expresses at the start of Romans 9.

Even though Paul has great anguish in his heart over the fate of his own countrymen, he does not let his emotional anguish lead him into disobedience. As he spends the following chapters explaining God's sovereignty in salvation and judgement and his work in history to reject the Jews and bring in the Gentiles, Paul acknowledges God's wisdom and right to act in any way he likes concerning his creation.

As we get into chapters 10 and 11 of Romans, we see Paul wrestling with the history of Israel. He realizes that, as terrible as it is, God's judgement on Israel is right because God has offered the Israelites grace and mercy over and over again, and they have rejected him over and over again in the stubbornness of their own hearts. Paul refuses to let his personal distress overwhelm or obscure what he knows about God, revealed in the gospel.

By the end of Romans 11 Paul has been so vividly reminded of God's righteousness, holiness and goodness that he cannot help but sing God's praises:

Oh, the depth of the riches and wisdom and knowledge of God! How unsearchable are his judgements and how inscrutable his ways!

> "For who has known the mind of the Lord,
>   or who has been his counselor?"
> "Or who has given a gift to him
>   that he might be repaid?"

For from him and through him and to him are all things. To him be glory forever. Amen. (Rom 11:33-36)

The God who created the world has loved the world at the cost of his own Son. He is a good and loving God. He is also righteous to judge and free to use his world as he wishes. Paul acknowledges the pain of watching his countrymen reject God, but he refuses to let it completely overwhelm him. He continues to search the Scriptures and wrestle with God's truth until he sees the wisdom and goodness of God.

As we suffer, we do well to continue to place ourselves in the way of truth—even truth that is sometimes hard to hear. Because in that truth we know our majestic God, whose glory is beyond knowing and whose goodness he will share with us in eternity.

SUFFERING WELL

Chapter 9

DOING GOOD WHILE SUFFERING

WHILE I'VE BEEN WRITING this book, several significant natural disasters have occurred in my part of the world. As I've already mentioned, Queensland has seen massive floods and the biggest cyclone to hit the Australian coast in a hundred years. And, just this week, an earthquake has struck Christchurch on the southern island of New Zealand. At this moment the death toll stands at 78, but it may be a couple of hundred by the time they finish digging the bodies out. Creation groans again.

The media reports of these events have revealed the massive variety of responses from people in the face of disaster. Some people sit quietly on the side of the road, absent and detached. Some weep and scream. Some make dry jokes and set about the dirty work of cleaning up. Some get angry at the authorities for their loss, seeking someone to blame in the hope that it might lessen the pain a little. As people search for words to describe what they have seen and experienced, hardly anyone is able to find an unused superlative. There is no way to make sense of such immense tragedy.

This all raises the obvious question: how should Christians react when we suffer? So far we have spent much of our time exploring what the Bible has to say about suffering. But as we experience suffering, we need to be equipped not just to think rightly about suffering but also to act rightly in the face of it. As God's people, what should we do when life hurts?

Praise God

The first step is to continue to praise God, and the challenge is to do it with integrity. It is worth thinking about what this might look like.

I am sure you have seen people praising God, as it were, through gritted teeth. In their shock and distress, they plaster on a smile and almost act as if nothing has happened. "God is good", they say, willing themselves to believe it even as they speak from their convictions. They may sound artificial but we must be careful before we condemn them for it. Grief and stress do strange things to us all.

The problem with almost all human behaviour is that it is complex and hard to understand. The significance of two identical actions can be worlds apart. In the face of difficulty, is someone's declaration of God's goodness their attempt to express convictions worked in them by God's Spirit that they are struggling to feel, or is it their attempt to look good in the eyes of others? Or is it a little of both, plus some other possibility we have not even thought of yet? It is very hard for us to know our own hearts, let alone the inner motivations of other people's hearts!

Take one of the Bible's great examples of godliness in the face of suffering. When Job's wife calls on him to "Curse God and die", he responds by saying to her, "You speak as one of the foolish women would speak. Shall we receive good from God, and shall we not receive evil?" The writer of Job tells us that "In all this Job did not sin with his lips" (2:9-10). Yet we do not really know what was in his heart or how he said it. Was he resigned, angry, perplexed, confident, or a little of all of these? In the rest of the book, Job shows that he is a man wrestling with his convictions. It takes a face-to-face meeting with God to clarify his commitment.

When we call on ourselves to praise God even in the face of suffering, we are seeking to do something that is very difficult and which we can only do by the grace of God's Spirit. It's important therefore to remember what 'praise' is. The idea of 'praise' is often reduced to singing a particular style of somewhat up-tempo music, but this is far from its biblical origin. In the Bible, to praise God is to declare his goodness to others. When the psalmists call on Israel to praise God, they invite the people to tell anyone who will listen about what their God is like. Israel praises God by recounting his great deeds in the Exodus and by speaking of his faithfulness to his promises.

How can we praise God with integrity in the face of suffering? By remembering the heart of God's goodness.

By remembering the way God has made himself known in Jesus. We are able to say God is good, because we know his love in Jesus Christ. We can tell people that God is worthy of their honour, because he has loved us and forgiven us at great cost and because he has promised in Jesus' resurrection that he will one day take away all suffering. We will praise God as we sing and speak of these things and as we strive to remember them and hold them in our hearts.

For me and for many others, music can be a particularly helpful gift from God in this regard. Music that expresses the deep truths of the faith can help us to hold on to and proclaim our trust in God, even when we are finding it difficult to do so. I've found two songs particularly helpful in trying to express a right confidence in God in the face of suffering. One is Matt Redman's 'Blessed be your name'. I remember singing it at the funeral for a small baby who had died in utero. With tears streaming down their faces, that little child's parents declared what they believed, even as they acknowledged the difficulty of the situation:

> You give and take away,
> You give and take away,
> My heart will choose to say,
> Lord, blessed be your name.[11]

---

11 Matt and Beth Redman, 'Blessed be your name', from the album *Where Angels Fear to Tread*, Survivor Records, 2002.

The other song is by an Australian musician, Colin Buchanan, who writes songs for children. It is a wonderful song that reminds me that God is on his throne ruling the world, even when the world does not seem right. I remember listening to it several times the night we learned that my father-in-law had a brain tumour. He passed away just over a year later.

> You might have seen bad things happening on the TV
> news,
> You might be worried about the world and what will
> happen to you,
> Put your trust in God alone,
> Cause he's still sitting on his mighty throne.
>
> The Lord is king, he's gonna look after everything,
> everything
> The Lord is king, he's gonna look after everything,
> Every single thing in this world, cause this is his world.
>
> You might get sad and wonder why there's so much pain,
> Why we let the same mistakes happen over and over
> again,
> Sinful ways will always fail,
> But God and his ways will prevail.
>
> Because the Lord is king, he's gonna look after
> everything, everything...[12]

---

12 Colin Buchanan, 'The Lord is king', from the album *10, 9, 8... God is Great*, Wanaaring Road Music, 2002.

God's good gift of music is able to minister to our spirits and remind us of truth, even in the midst of great sadness—especially when gifted musicians have managed to capture an aspect of God's biblical revelation. Music can also help us to express great truths that need to be expressed when we struggle to feel them.

As we seek to speak well of God in the midst of anguish, there is one more truth we should remember: stoicism is not a Christian virtue. Stoicism was a Greek philosophical school that taught people to seek moral and intellectual perfection by having no emotions. But the Bible doesn't call on us to be unemotional. God created us as emotional beings; it's right to rejoice and right to mourn. Paul's words to the Thessalonians are a good example: he does not tell them to cease grieving over the loved ones they have lost. But he does encourage them to grieve differently from those who have no hope (1 Thess 4:13).

When we face difficulty, it is right to cry. God created us to feel and express pain. But the Spirit has remade us in the image of Jesus as those who are also able to declare the goodness of God in Christ, even when our pain is very great. When we suffer, we ought to prayerfully ask God to help us continue to praise him—to declare that we know our God is good and heaven is our home.

Do good

Praising God is not all God asks of us in the face of suffering. God also calls on his people, in all of the circumstances of life, to do good. In fact, doing good is at the heart of the Christian life.

When Jesus lived and died and rose again for us, what was his purpose? The Bible expresses it in many ways. It was to forgive our sins. It was to bring glory to his Father. It was to bring us hope. But one of the things the Bible speaks about often is Jesus' purpose in transforming his people to do good. Listen to how the following passages put it:

> For the grace of God has appeared, bringing salvation for all people, training us to renounce ungodliness and worldly passions, and to live self-controlled, upright, and godly lives in the present age, waiting for our blessed hope, the appearing of the glory of our great God and Saviour Jesus Christ, who gave himself for us to redeem us from all lawlessness and to purify for himself a people for his own possession who are zealous for good works. (Titus 2:11-14)

> For we are [God's] workmanship, created in Christ Jesus for good works, which God prepared beforehand, that we should walk in them. (Eph 2:10)

Paul tells the Colossians that he prays for them to "walk in a manner worthy of the Lord... bearing fruit in every good work and increasing in the knowledge of God" (Col 1:10). He prays for the Thessalonians, "that our God may make you worthy of his calling and may fulfil every resolve for good and every work of faith by his power" (2 Thess 1:11). He encourages Titus to remind the people "to devote themselves to good works" (Titus 3:14), and Hebrews tells us to "stir up one another to love and good works" (Heb 10:24).

God's purpose in Christ was not just to forgive us (as wonderful as that is) but also to transform us into new people who love the deeds of light rather than the deeds of darkness. And as we have already seen, God grants us the incredible privilege of living in such a way that we bring glory to him. That's why, when Peter writes to those suffering persecution, he encourages them to keep doing good:

> Beloved, I urge you as sojourners and exiles to abstain from the passions of the flesh, which wage war against your soul. Keep your conduct among the Gentiles honourable, so that when they speak against you as evildoers, they may see your good deeds and glorify God on the day of visitation. (1 Pet 2:11-12)

> Therefore let those who suffer according to God's will entrust their souls to a faithful Creator while doing good. (1 Pet 4:19)

When we suffer, we need to have Jesus' words ringing in our ears:

> "You are the light of the world. A city set on a hill cannot be hidden. Nor do people light a lamp and put it under a basket, but on a stand, and it gives light to all in the house. In the same way, let your light shine before others, so that they may see your good works and give glory to your Father who is in heaven." (Matt 5:14-16)

Here again, we encounter an unnatural response to suffering, a response that may seem harsh: "Stop moaning and do good!" But that's not what God is saying. If we listen carefully we will hear something entirely different. When Peter writes to urge his readers to do good, he knows it will be difficult for them. He knows it may even cause them more pain. But he's convinced that God's purpose in the death and resurrection of Jesus is good for us. Why do we seek to do good in the face of suffering? It is because God has made us a new creation in Christ; it is because doing good is what God would do. In fact, it's exactly what he **did** do. And it is what God's people have done ever since.

I work on a large university campus in Sydney. In God's kindness, we see students come to the campus from all over the world. Every year, men and women come from China, Malaysia, Indonesia, Singapore and Hong Kong—often at great expense to their families— to earn a degree and return home. Many of them come from families and cultures that have been entirely unaffected by the gospel. But while in Australia, many of them meet Christians and hear of God's love in Jesus. Some of them turn to Christ. Some of them then go on to consider missionary service for Jesus' sake.

For many of these brothers and sisters in Christ, the decision to follow Jesus comes at great personal cost. They ring their parents only to be shouted at for destroying the family name and throwing away the investment that has been made in them. I have seen parents fly out to Australia at a moment's notice in order to try and stop their children being baptized. They apply all sorts of emotional and financial pressure. I have sat and prayed through tears with those who are crying because their families have done everything but abandon them.

But the true work of the Spirit is wondrous to behold. Over and over again, I have seen these young Christians continue to love their families. Rather than stay in Australia for holidays, they go home to be with those who make their lives miserable, knowing they will be ridiculed or verbally abused or given the silent treatment. When they go home they go out of their way to serve. They help with the housework, they make meals, they remember family birthdays, and they bear the brunt of caring for younger siblings. Back here in Australia, they often manage households where they cook and clean to help when their siblings come to study. They ring home every week, even though the conversations are often strained and joyless. They do it because they love their families and want to see them come to know Christ as well.

It is a supernatural grace that allows these brothers and sisters to respond with grace and love in the face of hostility and anger. Their lives are an encouragement and a rebuke. They know what it means to respond to suffering by doing good.

Whether our suffering is the general suffering of living in this fallen world or the particular suffering of belonging to Jesus, God encourages us to respond to our pain not with self-pity, but by doing good.

Wait patiently

There is a third thing the Scriptures encourage us to do when life becomes hard: nothing at all. God calls on those who suffer to wait patiently for his justice and his time.

The Thessalonian Christians were an example to other believers because they responded to the gospel by waiting:

> And you became imitators of us and of the Lord, for you received the word in much affliction, with the joy of the Holy Spirit, so that you became an example to all the believers in Macedonia and in Achaia. For not only has the word of the Lord sounded forth from you in Macedonia and Achaia, but your faith in God has gone forth everywhere, so that we need not say anything. For they themselves report concerning us the kind of reception we had among you, and how you turned to God from idols to serve the living and true God, and to wait for his Son from heaven, whom he raised from the dead, Jesus who delivers us from the wrath to come. (1 Thess 1:6-10)

Jesus taught his disciples to respond to those who persecuted them not by retaliating, but by patiently doing good to their enemies:

> "You have heard that it was said, 'An eye for an eye and a tooth for a tooth.' But I say to you, Do not resist the one who is evil. But if anyone slaps you on the right cheek, turn to him the other also. And if anyone would sue you and take your tunic, let him have your cloak as well. And if anyone forces you to go one mile, go with him two miles. Give to the one who begs from you, and do not refuse the one who would borrow from you.
>
> "You have heard that it was said, 'You shall love your neighbour and hate your enemy.' But I say to you, Love your enemies and pray for those who

persecute you, so that you may be sons of your Father who is in heaven. For he makes his sun rise on the evil and on the good, and sends rain on the just and on the unjust." (Matt 5:38-45)

We live in a world that doesn't like waiting. When we get ill, we want someone to fix it—quickly. Indeed, we are often surprised when medical professionals can't help. We have the technology—surely something can be done! When we want to eat, we expect to be served immediately. Fast food is everywhere, and it must be **fast**. In a world that wants everything fixed yesterday, the Bible commends waiting in the strongest possible terms.

Why? It is because waiting teaches us about the nature of our God and of ourselves. When we're forced to wait rather than being able to solve a problem, we're reminded who actually controls the world. For all of our human ingenuity, there is so much we cannot do. We can build bridges, but we cannot always stop earthquakes from destroying them. We can cure many illnesses, but death is still the end of us all. The gospel's call to wait patiently is a reminder of a truth we often fail to acknowledge: that all life comes from God's hand.

"The God who made the world and everything in it, being Lord of heaven and earth, does not live in temples made by man, nor is he served by human hands, as though he needed anything, since he himself gives to all mankind life and breath and everything. And he made from one man every nation of mankind to live on all the face of the earth, having determined allotted periods and the boundaries of their dwelling place, that they should seek God, and perhaps feel their way toward him and find him." (Acts 17:24-27)

In a world built for speed, the gospel challenges us to be patient. Learning to accept our finitude is part of becoming humble and submissive servants. In some ways, this is the challenge of all suffering. We know God has promised us an eternal home—a place where we will not struggle with sin, and where the blackness of death will never be seen. We long for our home and we cry out for God to deliver us. But we are called to wait. God will deliver his future when he is ready and not according to our timetable. This is part of what it means for God to be God and for us to be creatures.

What are Christians called to do in the face of suffering? We are called to wait well, to praise our God in every moment, and to ask for God's strength to do good—even to our enemies. Our goal is that Jesus might be glorified and that our Father might be all in all (1 Cor 15:28).

Chapter 10

THE MISSING PIECE
OF THE PUZZLE

On a recent family holiday we stayed at a friend's beach house. One of the fun things about going to someone else's place is exploring their books and games and puzzles. To our great delight we found a huge *Where's Wally?* puzzle in the cupboard. It became our holiday project. In between trips to the beach and the fish and chip shop, various family members would stand around the table matching pieces and talking (mainly about the puzzle, but it was family communication nonetheless!).

Day by day as the pieces came together, the picture slowly materialized before our eyes. But as the end drew near, we realized we were going to be disappointed— we were missing a piece! For some families, this would simply be a minor disappointment. But in a family of A-type personalities, it verged on a national disaster. No matter how good the rest of the picture was, we needed that last piece to rejoice in the whole. Fortunately, after much searching under furniture, we eventually found the piece. The puzzle was complete.

We've pieced together many of the biblical truths about suffering, but one significant piece is still missing. It has been lying there on the table, and from time to time we've glanced at it. But if we're going to think God's thoughts about suffering, the missing piece needs to take its place in the centre of the picture. That piece is labelled 'Hope', and on it is pictured the restoration of all things at Jesus' return.

If we are going to learn to suffer well, we need to contemplate the hope that God holds out in the gospel—and rejoice!

The heart of our hope

Where do we start? Perhaps a little strangely, we start with the place of human beings in God's world. Our world displays the glory and shame of humanity every day. The nightly news is a bizarre mix of sin's awfulness and the wonder of God's general grace. As I write, Colonel Gaddafi's ridiculous ravings fill my screen. The Libyan dictator insists he has led the country well and his people have experienced only the best under his leadership—even though his soldiers are now killing hundreds as he attempts to hold on to power. Yet in the very next story, I see scenes of generosity and bravery as people try to rescue survivors from the rubble in the aftermath of the huge earthquake in Christchurch.

We are curious creatures—capable of so much evil and such great altruism. And reading the Bible only amplifies the mystery of our double nature:

> When I look at your heavens, the work of your fingers,
>> the moon and the stars, which you have set in place,
> what is man that you are mindful of him,
>> and the son of man that you care for him?
>
> Yet you have made him a little lower than the heavenly
>> beings
>> and crowned him with glory and honour.
> You have given him dominion over the works of your
>> hands;
>> you have put all things under his feet,
> all sheep and oxen,
>> and also the beasts of the field,
> the birds of the heavens, and the fish of the sea,
>> whatever passes along the paths of the seas.
>> (Ps 8:3-8)

As David reflects in this psalm on the nature of human beings, two things stand out. On the one hand is our obscurity and finitude. Why should the God who made the universe and set the stars in place care about us? We are like ants, scurrying around, gathering and consuming our little lives away while desperately trying to ignore the grave that awaits us. Why should God bother with our petty rebellion, let alone share his glory with us?

And yet something else also stands out in Psalm 8.

The God who made the world also made people like

us to rule the world. He gave dominion over his creation to us. You would not necessarily know it from looking at the world, but God has crowned humanity with glory and honour. And, even more remarkably, God has tied the future of this creation to the fate of human beings:

> For the creation waits with eager longing for the revealing of the sons of God. For the creation was subjected to futility, not willingly, but because of him who subjected it, in hope that the creation itself will be set free from its bondage to corruption and obtain the freedom of the glory of the children of God.
> (Rom 8:19-21)

Just as God set creation under our feet in the beginning—"Be fruitful and multiply and fill the earth and subdue it, and have dominion over the fish of the sea and over the birds of the heavens and over every living thing that moves on the earth" (Gen 1:28)—so he cursed it because of our failure: "Cursed is the ground because of you; in pain you shall eat of it all the days of your life; thorns and thistles it shall bring forth for you" (Gen 3:17-18). Yet, as Romans 8 tells us, God will one day liberate the whole universe from its bondage to decay by restoring his children in glory.

While the world tells us that human beings are just another part of the food chain, God tells us that humanity is the centrepiece of his plan. By God's grace, we are precious to him. And throughout human history, God has worked towards the glorious future he has planned for us in spite of the sin that characterizes us. When Adam and Eve sinned, they were expelled from the garden but not destroyed. When the world was wicked in the days of Noah, God chose to rescue humanity through Noah and his family. In the face of the tower of Babel, God promised Abraham that through his descendants, every nation would be blessed. And in spite of the repeated, unrepentant rebellion of Israel that caused them to be cast from the Promised Land, God continued to promise a future to Israel and, through Israel, a future for the whole world.

We shouldn't be surprised by God's grace in the face of sin. After all, he planned from before the world's creation to send Jesus in the likeness of sinful people. But can you see how our fate is connected to Jesus' fate? In God's plan, Jesus' glory is tied up with becoming human. God made us to rule the world so he could send his Son in our likeness to be the true human who will rule the new creation. God's plan was to glorify his Son by working through him to share the Son's rule and glory with us. Because of Jesus' work, we will one day stand with him—our brother and great high priest—ruling over the new heavens and the new earth. And this all accords with the plan that God established before time began.

And so at the very heart of our hope lies the unchanging character of God. God promised to make a people for himself, and he achieved it in the most remarkable way possible: by sending his only Son into the world as a person. In the man Jesus Christ, God both fulfilled all of his Old Testament prophecies—"all the promises of God find their Yes in him" (2 Cor 1:20)—and guaranteed our future.

When it comes to persevering and growing in the face

of suffering, this is one of the greatest encouragements the New Testament offers. If God has planned for humans to rule the world with Jesus, and if he has gone so far as to send his Son into the world to be mocked, reviled and crucified for our sake, then we can be certain about the future. Hear Paul's words in Romans:

> Therefore, since we have been justified by faith, we have peace with God through our Lord Jesus Christ. Through him we have also obtained access by faith into this grace in which we stand, and we rejoice in hope of the glory of God. Not only that, but we rejoice in our sufferings, knowing that suffering produces endurance, and endurance produces character, and character produces hope, and hope does not put us to shame, because God's love has been poured into our hearts through the Holy Spirit who has been given to us.
>
> For while we were still weak, at the right time Christ died for the ungodly. For one will scarcely die for a righteous person—though perhaps for a good person one would dare even to die—but God shows his love for us in that while we were still sinners, Christ died for us. Since, therefore, we have now been justified by his blood, much more shall we be saved by him from the wrath of God. For if while we were enemies we were reconciled to God by the death of his Son, much more, now that we are reconciled, shall we be saved by his life. More than that, we also rejoice in God through our Lord Jesus Christ, through whom we have now received reconciliation. (Rom 5:1-11)

If God has done the difficult thing of sending Jesus to die

for his enemies, how much more can we be certain of the future knowing that Jesus has been raised to life as the Lord of all! We can rejoice in our sufferings because God has given us a hope that won't be put to shame. The hope is that Christ died our death for sin, and his life is ours.

This is the very great significance of the doctrine of union with Christ. Those who have become a part of Christ through the work of his Holy Spirit and through hearing the gospel are so much a part of him that what is his is now ours: "If we have been united with him in a death like his, we shall certainly be united with him in a resurrection like his" (Rom 6:5).

Paul describes it to the Corinthians by pointing to Jesus as the last Adam. Of course, Jesus and Adam are quite different from each other—some might say totally opposite. But Jesus is like Adam in one very important way: all who belong to him are affected completely and totally by him.

> But in fact Christ has been raised from the dead,
> the firstfruits of those who have fallen asleep. For as
> by a man came death, by a man has come also the
> resurrection of the dead. For as in Adam all die, so
> also in Christ shall all be made alive. But each in his
> own order: Christ the firstfruits, then at his coming
> those who belong to Christ. (1 Cor 15:20-23)

Christ's resurrection is the promise of a harvest to come. Our bodies, planted as seeds in the grave, will one day flower and bear fruit as resurrection bodies. The earth dropped on our coffins is preparing us to grow in ways beyond our ability to imagine. We will receive new selves, fit to inherit eternity. What is corrupt will be made incorruptible. What is weak will be filled with God's power. What is dishonourable will be raised in glory. And this is all guaranteed by Jesus' work for us.

But what exactly is it that Jesus guarantees? What will heavenly life be like? Christ's resurrection body points us towards the nature of life in the new heavens and the new earth. Heaven is not a harp-playing cloud holiday, but a feast of all the goodness of creation enjoyed in the fellowship of believers with our God. The world to come is not white and fluffy but physical and real—rich with colours beyond the ability of any HD television to reproduce. Trees bearing the most exquisite fruits will surround the river of life. We will enjoy life in the light of the glory of the living God. We will know God fully, even as we are already fully known (1 Cor 13:12).

What is our hope? **It is that God will do what he has promised**. And it is a certain hope, because through Jesus God has already fulfilled all his promises, even as he makes a new promise: to bring us home to live in glory with him. In Christ we know that God forgives our sin, adopts us as his children and makes a room in his house that we will occupy with joy for all eternity (John 14:1-3).

These truths are crucial to comprehend and savour, if we are to learn to suffer well. They were the truths that compelled the apostle Paul to live for Christ in the face of even death itself. "To live is Christ, and to die is gain" (Phil 1:21)—Paul could declare this with confidence because he saw the risen Jesus, and he reflected on the nature of his promise-keeping God. Having consumed these truths and digested them into his being, he was able to live for Christ and Christ alone:

> But whatever gain I had, I counted as loss for the
> sake of Christ. Indeed, I count everything as loss
> because of the surpassing worth of knowing Christ
> Jesus my Lord. For his sake I have suffered the loss
> of all things and count them as rubbish, in order that
> I may gain Christ and be found in him, not having
> a righteousness of my own that comes from the law,
> but that which comes through faith in Christ, the
> righteousness from God that depends on faith—that
> I may know him and the power of his resurrection,
> and may share his sufferings, becoming like him in
> his death, that by any means possible I may attain the
> resurrection from the dead. (Phil 3:7-11)

Paul would endure anything, suffer anything, persevere in everything—because he knew this world was not his home.

Could you say the same thing about us?

Human ingenuity has resulted in a level of wealth that enables us to amuse ourselves to death. Life is comfortable and the pleasures of modernity are enticing. iPhones, computerized cars, surround-sound entertainment, food from the four corners of the world... We have more than enough to keep most of us entertained, and certainly enough to distract us from thinking about the future and about death. Paul would say these things are rubbish—worthless scraps to be discarded in the face of the coming treasures of heavenly life. But we feel the tug of the world so keenly. Why should we suffer for Christ, when this world is so enjoyable? Couldn't we have Christ and enjoy all the comfort of this world too?

Here, surely, is the source of the double-mindedness that affects so many of us. Our world doesn't believe in heaven. In fact, it teaches us that the only heaven available is the one we make for ourselves. Let us eat and drink, for tomorrow we die.

In our folly, we believe it. I remember talking a number of years ago to a young medical student who was thinking about the possibility of missionary service. As we talked, he was refreshingly (if sadly) honest: "I know God's glory matters. I know people need to hear about Jesus Christ. I know my own comfort isn't everything. But what if it's all a lie? What if Christ didn't really die? What if God isn't really there? I'd have given up everything for nothing."

I think he said what many of us harbour in our hearts but are fearful to say. We are secretly worried the world might be right. We have lost sight of heaven. We have let go of God's promises. We live with a foot in both camps, afraid to leave Christ behind but terrified of what might happen if we wholeheartedly planted both feet at the foot of the cross.

The solution is to turn again to the display of God's love in Jesus Christ. If we are to suffer well, we must remind ourselves of God's promises fulfilled in Christ. We must teach each other about the importance of the resurrection and the future that God has in store for us.

SUFFERING WELL

It is only as the things of this world are dimmed by the glory of God that we will be able to live and to suffer for Christ, becoming so like him in his death that God will bring us to share in his resurrection (Phil 3:8-11).

This is the hope God brings us in Christ. It is the hope we must keep sharing with each other. It is the hope to which we ask God to enable us to cling. It is the one true hope for all people everywhere. It is our hope!

Chapter 11

SUFFERING WELL

About ten years ago I was involved in a pastor's training conference. In one session, as we talked about discipling young believers, we tried to come up with a list of key biblical truths we would want to teach every new Christian. People gave the usual responses (and that's not a bad thing!): we wanted to teach new Christians the importance of Jesus' death in our place; we wanted them to know about the Holy Spirit's work; we wanted them to understand sin; we wanted to teach them about church. But then a woman who had been a missionary in Argentina for many years added her voice to the conversation. I will never forget her contribution: "We need to teach them to suffer".

In my ungodliness, this had not occurred to me as a crucial thing to teach a new convert. But she was completely right. The New Testament is full of encouragement to understand suffering from God's perspective and to suffer well. The problem with the ideas presented in this book is that they are so quick to read over, yet they take so long to take root in our souls. There are more pleasant topics to teach about than suffering, so Bible teachers often neglect to prepare people well to live for Christ.

In this final chapter I want to summarize the key ideas we've seen, and suggest some ways forward in preparing ourselves to suffer well. These will not be definitive, but my hope is that they'll help you begin to think creatively about how we can grow in suffering well for Christ.

Trust God and do good

Perhaps the most crucial thing to take away from reading this book is a determination to read the Bible biblically rather than according to our cultural norms. We need to know God on God's terms. To that end, let's remember the core of the New Testament teaching about suffering. It is perhaps best summarized by Paul's words at the beginning of 2 Corinthians:

> Blessed be the God and Father of our Lord Jesus
> Christ, the Father of mercies and God of all comfort,
> who comforts us in all our affliction, so that we may
> be able to comfort those who are in any affliction, with
> the comfort with which we ourselves are comforted
> by God. For as we share abundantly in Christ's
> sufferings, so through Christ we share abundantly in
> comfort too. If we are afflicted, it is for your comfort
> and salvation; and if we are comforted, it is for your
> comfort, which you experience when you patiently
> endure the same sufferings that we suffer. Our hope

for you is unshaken, for we know that as you share in
our sufferings, you will also share in our comfort.
(2 Cor 1:3-7)

Paul wants to comfort the suffering Corinthians with the same comfort he has received from God. Paul doesn't go into great detail about what that comfort is but he makes one very clear statement, which summarizes much of what we have seen: "As we share abundantly in Christ's sufferings, so through Christ we share abundantly in comfort too". Whatever the comfort Paul wants to share with the Corinthians, it is the comfort that comes from so belonging to Jesus that we suffer for him.

In order to appreciate what that means, we need to reassess our definitions of comfort once more. As I drive south out of Sydney, I pass by The Comfort Shop on a semi-regular basis. The sole purpose of The Comfort Shop is to get me to part with thousands of dollars for the experience of perfect bodily comfort. I could buy a motorized leather reclining chair, or a bed designed by chiropractors to give me the closest experience possible to sleeping in the clouds while making my back better than ever before. Comfort in our world involves money and luxury and soft pillows and feeling like a prince or a princess for a while.

But these things are nothing like what the Bible means by comfort. What is the comfort Paul has as he suffers for Christ? If we have read the rest of the New Testament correctly, it is the comfort of belonging to the king who owns and rules the world. It is the encouragement of knowing that whatever happens in this world, it happens under the hand of a sovereign God who is forming Paul's character to be like Jesus. It is the hope of knowing that God is shaping him to inherit eternity. It is the joy of knowing that he is living for righteousness' sake—that his life will bring glory and honour and praise to his saviour at Jesus' return.

Or, as Paul puts it in the next paragraph in 2 Corinthians, it is the comfort of knowing the God who raises the dead:

> For we do not want you to be unaware, brothers, of the affliction we experienced in Asia. For we were so utterly burdened beyond our strength that we despaired of life itself. Indeed, we felt that we had received the sentence of death. But that was to make us rely not on ourselves but on God who raises the dead. He delivered us from such a deadly peril, and he will deliver us. On him we have set our hope that he will deliver us again. (2 Cor 1:8-10)

If we were to summarize the New Testament's teaching on suffering, we might put it like this:

Live such good lives for the Lord Jesus Christ that the world will hate you for it. And when the suffering comes, whatever happens, entrust yourself to God and continue to do good, knowing that God will one day raise you from the dead.

That is the Bible's message about suffering. That is what it means to suffer well.

At the heart of learning to suffer well, then, is remembering Jesus—the author and perfector of our faith. He is the one who teaches us what it means to despise the shame of the world's hatred (Heb 12:2). He is the one who shows us how to trust God and do good, even when it hurts. But more than that, he is also God's promise that all those who belong to him will see their heavenly home. In Christ's death and resurrection we see our own glorious future.

How can we work at remembering and rejoicing in that future while living good and godly lives in the here and now? As I've suggested in the rest of the book, it will involve understanding God as he shows himself to us in his word. How do we do that? Here are a few suggestions.

Getting practical

If we want to trust God and suffer well, we need to begin by **knowing** the God in whom we are placing our trust—the God who is the sovereign Lord over all his creation. The seemingly mundane but radically life-changing way in which this comes about is by listening to what God has to say to us. And so we must learn again what it means to be students of God's word.

Primarily this will mean reading lots of the Bible—and in particular, those parts we often avoid. One example that springs to mind is the importance of going on to study Romans 9-11 rather than ending every Bible study series at the end of Romans 8 because we're a bit worried about arguments over predestination.

But the bigger issue, I suspect, is that we need to work at learning to read the Old Testament.

For many of us, the Old Testament is slightly scary and difficult to understand. That's not particularly surprising. Sacrificing animals, obeying complex ceremonial laws and going to war in the Promised Land are not really part of our experience. This makes reading the Old Testament feel like hard work. But if we don't read it, we miss out on so much.

For example, a book like Isaiah lays out the character of God and teaches us so much about his relationship with creation. Books like Deuteronomy and Joshua challenge us to accept that God's sovereign control of the world includes the right to judge—God sent his people into the Promised Land to wipe out the nations because sin is terrible and worthy of judgement. And parts of the Bible like 2 Kings, Hosea and Lamentations teach us why God brought destruction on his own people.

The Old Testament helps us to think about things it's easier not to think about. Things like the sinfulness of humanity and the righteousness of God. These absolute truths are vital to understand if we are to rid ourselves of our world's endless relativity. God is good and we are not. We must read and pray and wrestle with this idea until we see our sin clearly, and God's righteousness even more clearly.

In very practical terms, this will involve setting aside time in our lives to read through the Bible. If you've never done it (and even if you have), why not find a yearly Bible reading plan that will encourage you to keep seeing all of God's revelation? And if you struggle to do it, why not work together with a group of Christian friends to help each other to keep reading? God's church family is one of his great blessings to us. You will find many rich rewards in helping each other to read more of God's word together.

As you read, you will no doubt encounter some big questions. So, on another very practical note, I'd like to commend Vaughan Robert's short book *God's Big Picture*.[13] This excellent overview teaches us how the Bible's story fits together so that you can make more sense of the Old Testament as you read it. In my pastoral experience, the joy of understanding how the whole Bible fits together has been a major turning point in the growth of many Christians I know.

If you prefer something more interactive, I suggest *The Bible Overview* course by Matthew Brain and Matthew Malcolm.[14] It summarizes the Bible's overarching story into 15 steps, providing a very valuable framework for understanding the Bible's individual parts. The course also provides a basic method for reading and understanding the Bible—a very handy little tool if you don't feel confident in your Bible reading.

Which leads us to the next big point: how you read the Bible is important. You can't really understand the Old Testament properly without understanding how it relates to Jesus. As much as the God of the Old Testament

---

13 IVP, Leicester, 2009.

14 Available from Matthias Media: www.matthiasmedia.com/rd.html?sku=the-bible-overview-course

is the same God we still worship today, the Bible tells us that the **fullness** of God is seen in Christ. Christ reveals more of God to us than the Old Testament does. In him we see the holy righteousness and generous compassion of our God. In Jesus we understand that God is good beyond our knowing. In Christ we see that judgement is right and real. In our Lord, we appreciate how God's sovereignty, judgement, grace, love and mercy come together in perfect display. So there is not an angry Old Testament God and a loving New Testament one, but simply one true God who has revealed the fullness of his character in his word and through his Son.

So, as we read the Old Testament we must also read the New Testament. We must keep letting the whole of the Scriptures speak together.

Which brings us to the most important point—a point I've already made a couple of times, but which is important enough to make again: in all of this we must **let the Bible say what it actually says**, rather than what we would like it to say. When you read something that seems really confusing or uncomfortable, don't just explain it away or brush it off. Think about it. Ask others about it. Read books about it. Ask your pastor about it. Wrestle with God's word and allow it to control your thinking—rather than controlling it with your thinking.

In particular—as I've been arguing all the way through—we need to think long and hard about why the New Testament spends so much time speaking about suffering for Jesus and so little time on suffering in a fallen world. Much folly has been spoken by proponents of the 'prosperity gospel', and even by well-meaning middle-class believers, on the topic of the goodness of the Christian life. So much of Western Christianity has taught people that Jesus will take their blues away. But Jesus says: blessed are you when men speak ill of you because you belong to me. We live in a Christian culture that has embraced the worldliness of our world and we have drunk deeply from the fountain of vain pleasure. But we will really begin to understand the joy of living for Christ only when we understand that belonging to Jesus involves living the resurrection life by joining him in suffering.

As we've seen, this doesn't mean all Christians will suddenly become martyrs. In God's kindness, our Christian history means that in many parts of the Western world we still experience great freedom to live for Christ. Most Christians in the West will not face death for their faith, or even imprisonment—at least not in the short term. But if we don't learn to do what is right and stand up for Jesus in the face of ridicule and reviling, what will we do if living for Christ becomes, once again, an issue for which you can be imprisoned?

By reading God's word—the Old and New Testaments together—we will remind ourselves that the call to be unashamed of Jesus, rather than being a minor biblical note, is a song sung with angelic gusto by Jesus and the apostolic chorus. Knowing this will help us to prayerfully wrestle with our aversion to rocking the boat. By the gracious work of God's Spirit, it will also teach us to become believers with the kind of backbone that God wants us to have.

Of course, one of the wonderful things about reading the whole Bible again and again is that we will also be reminded of the riches of our hope in Christ. In a world that promises heaven on earth, we seem to have slowly lost our grip on eternity. Perhaps if we were to suffer a little more, we might understand more deeply the promise of heavenly rest.

If you've missed the point so far, one of the key things to **do** if we want to suffer well is to read, mark, learn and inwardly digest the fullness of God's revelation. Don't just walk away from reading this chapter thinking it's a good idea. Stop now and work out when you can find time to read God's word, and work out a plan to keep exposing yourself to all of God's word.

Just do it

But of course (if I can say this without sounding heretical) just reading the Bible is not enough. The person who searches the Scriptures and fails to put them into practice is like the person who looks in a mirror and walks away only to forget how big their nose is. God's word calls us to obey him as we live in his world.

When we read Scripture, we see God as he really is and we see ourselves as we really are. One of God's great graces is that this knowledge changes us. So if we are to learn to suffer well, not only must we drink deeply from the river of life that flows forth from the pages of God's word, but we must also seek to live that word out. Practically, this must involve at least two things.

Firstly, it will involve meeting regularly with God's people and listening to those who are already living out his word. How great an encouragement it will be to all of us if we live out this truth together—if we are so committed to biblical truth that our families and workmates think we are a little strange for living so seriously for Jesus. We need to learn to tell each other the stories of our embarrassments: the difficulty of driving down the freeway at the speed limit while having people drive angrily on our tails; the sadness of being ostracized at work because we won't join in the smutty jokes; the pain of going to a family funeral where we won't join in false religious traditions; the effort of trying to tell our families about Jesus only to have them ignore us and tell stories behind our backs—again!

It is so easy to become weary of doing good—and the world will never encourage us to do it. We need to spur one another on to do those good works that God has prepared for us to do. Let's share our stories and laugh and cry together and pray for each other that next time we will be brave enough to stand up and live for Christ.

Of course, just talking about it with each other is only the first step. The second step is to actually do it. In this regard, I have seen great courage and boldness spring up in Christian students as they have made themselves do things they are scared about—like inviting a friend along to an event to learn about Jesus, or walking up to a stranger and trying to start a conversation about Christ, or door-knocking in residential colleges to see if people are willing to talk with them about the life-giving work of Jesus.

I've only met a few people out of a thousand who look forward to doing this with fearless joy. For most people, these activities come laced with great anxiety and deep personal fears. But for those who trust God and step outside of their comfort zone to honour Jesus and make him known, I invariably see great growth in Christian maturity. Why? It is because of God's faithfulness to his promises.

Remember what Jesus said:

> "If anyone would come after me, let him deny himself
> and take up his cross and follow me. For whoever
> would save his life will lose it, but whoever loses
> his life for my sake and the gospel's will save it."
> (Mark 8:34-35)

And what did he promise his disciples when they were worried about the cost of following him?

> "Truly, I say to you, there is no-one who has left house
> or brothers or sisters or mother or father or children
> or lands, for my sake and for the gospel, who will
> not receive a hundredfold now in this time, houses
> and brothers and sisters and mothers and children
> and lands, with persecutions, and in the age to come
> eternal life. But many who are first will be last, and the
> last first." (Mark 10:29-31)

The fundamental New Testament truth is that we still live in the age of darkness. Now is the time of suffering for those who want to belong to the light of the world. The challenge is: will we accept the shame of being lights in the darkness for a time, or will we give in to the world's darkness and miss out on the glorious light that is ours in Jesus? Will we live such good lives for the Lord Jesus Christ that the world will hate us for it? And when the suffering comes, will we entrust ourselves to God and continue to do good, knowing that he will one day raise us from the dead?

Gaining God's truths

In my own experience, there are no shortcuts to having these truths indwell our lives. For many years in my early Christian life, I longed for a moment of breakthrough. I earnestly sought one single blessed moment in God's presence that would free me from all my struggles. I asked God to do an instant work in me to make me like Jesus.

What I have learned over many years now is that joy in God's righteous truth comes about through his discipline. Those who aren't disciplined aren't real children. All the riches of Christ's character are worked in us over time as we learn God's truth and prayerfully seek to live it out. The elderly saints I know who long for their heavenly home have come to do so by God's good gift of suffering and the work of his Spirit in their lives. This work didn't take place in one single moment of discovery, but over years of prayerful study of God's word (marked by many precious moments of discovery).

My prayer is that this book might spur you on to know God—to know him as he truly is and to live in the light of his generous revelation. It is a lifelong task, through which God will shape you to be like his Son. May we stand in glory together, singing the praises of our wondrous Lord, who by his power enables us to scorn the shame of living for Christ for the joy he sets before us.

May we come to the end of our life and hear our saviour say, "Well done my good and faithful servant. You have suffered well."

Feedback on this resource

We really appreciate getting feedback about our resources—not just suggestions for how to improve them, but also positive feedback and ways they can be used. We especially love to hear that the resources may have helped someone in their Christian growth.

You can send feedback to us via the 'Feedback' menu in our online store, or write to us at PO Box 225, Kingsford NSW 2032, Australia.

Matthias Media is an evangelical publishing ministry that seeks to persuade all Christians of the truth of God's purposes in Jesus Christ as revealed in the Bible, and equip them with high-quality resources, so that by the work of the Holy Spirit they will:

- abandon their lives to the honour and service of Christ in daily holiness and decision-making
- pray constantly in Christ's name for the fruitfulness and growth of his gospel
- speak the Bible's life-changing word whenever and however they can—in the home, in the world and in the fellowship of his people.

It was in 1988 that we first started pursuing this mission, and in God's kindness we now have more than 300 different ministry resources being used all over the world. These resources range from Bible studies and books through to training courses and audio sermons.

To find out more about our large range of very useful resources, and to access samples and free downloads, visit our website:

www.matthiasmedia.com

How to buy our resources

1. Direct from us over the internet:
  – in the US: www.matthiasmedia.com
  – in Australia and the rest of the world: www.matthiasmedia.com.au
2. Direct from us by phone:
  – in the US: 1 866 407 4530
  – in Australia: 1800 814 360 (Sydney: 9663 1478)
  – international: +61-2-9663-1478

> Register at our website for our **free** regular email update to receive information about the latest new resources **exclusive special offers**, and free articles to help you grow in your Christian life and ministry.

3. Through a range of outlets in various parts of the world. Visit **www.matthiasmedia.com/contact** for details about recommended retailers in your part of the world, including www.thegoodbook.co.uk in the United Kingdom.
4. Trade enquiries can be addressed to:
  – in the US and Canada: sales@matthiasmedia.com
  – in Australia and the rest of the world: sales@matthiasmedia.com.au

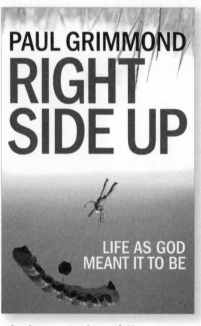